New Expanded Second Edition

SAY "YES" TO LOVE
God Explains SoulMates
Through
Yaël and Doug Powell

Circle of Light Press
Eureka Springs, Arkansas

Say 'Yes' To Love,
God Explains SoulMates
Through Yaël and Doug Powell

Copyright ©2001 by Yaël and Doug Powell
Second Edition 2003

Paperback Original ISBN 0-9725991-0-X
Circle of Light Press

Yaël and Doug Powell
Circle of Light
3969 Mundell Road
Eureka Springs, AR 72631

Cover design and book layout by Judith Bicking
Compilation, editing of Messages by Shanna Mac Lean
Art work by Yaël Powell

web site: www.circleoflight.net
email: connect@circleoflight.net

Printing: InstantPublisher.com Collierville, TN

SAY 'YES' TO LOVE SERIES
Through Yaël and Doug Powell
Circle of Light Press

Say "Yes" to Love, God Explains SoulMates

Say "Yes" to Love, God Unveils
SoulMate Love and Sacred Sexuality

Say "Yes" to Love, God's Guidance to LightWorkers

Soon to be published

Say "Yes" to Love, God Leads Humanity
Toward Christ Consciousness

Say "Yes" to Love, Giving Birth to the Christ Light

WORDS FROM OUR READERS

"I proceed very slowly reading these Messages because it's as if it weren't my eyes that were reading it, but my heart. It's as if I've just come Home. Your Messages are so "soft." I don't know how else to describe them. It feels like being wrapped in something very delicate. I keep crying all the time when I read them... I feel so very beloved." Paula Launonen, Ravenna, Italy

"Words are so inadequate to describe how these books have touched my life, especially **God Explains SoulMates.** It's what I always thought relationships can be, and I never found it put into black and white. Here it was, so perfectly described. I devoured it like I would the finest 'crème brulé,' not stopping until I had every last morsel of it, and then craved for more. It came at a time when I had said to my friends, 'I found my Twin Flame,' never knowing what it meant. Now I know." Carol Davis, Cat Spring, Texas

"Reading the Messages from God is like communing with God. Even if they are addressed to all humanity, they can also be a very personal experience. When you read the Messages from God, your heart will open and stay open if you so choose. A cascade of sparkling, fresh, flowing, colored Love energy. In Love from Love to Love creating more Love. I will be thankful forever." Tiziana Paggiolu, London, England

"Everything in the Messages resonates so deeply in me. I am amazed that I've found so much that had already been revealed to me in visions and dreams...it sometimes takes my breath away! It has given so much validity to everything I had already come to believe. Thank you all for feeling the need to share the Messages. They have meant so much to me in my journey. It's kind of like piloting a boat by the stars and one day discovering a secret compartment full of maps that show where all the ports of call are located. It makes it so much easier to get where you want to go!" Diane Dunville, Lanexa, VA

"In all my study, discernment, and spiritual practice over the years, I found that each teaching was only a step, only part of the process. I have known that each of us is so much more than our limited experiences have shown us. I seemed to need the bigger picture. I began to believe that I just was not ready or open enough to receive this divine manifestation. Then came *Say 'YES' to Love*. That grace, that grandness, that confirmation that we are so much more than we can ever imagine sang out to me boldly. The whole of co-creation was simplified and resonated fully within me. The consistent theme is that we are truly only Love and are much more than we can now comprehend. *Say 'YES' to Love* is also very practical — most notably in how to function in a world of duality when you know only Love is real. Just as the pressure of others' duality began eroding my knowing, this book arrived to help gently guide me. Just as Creator promised." Peggy Zetler, Dillon, Montana.

"These Messages are stunning, clear, beautiful, re-activating, stirring to the core of my being. This material reminds me of Home, reminds me to express the totality of my being, reminds me of how close to Home we are now, reminds me of my Twin Flame. Just having the books and knowing their content is a small sign of the ecstasy to come." Karen Porrit, U.K.

"These Messages, faithfully documented by Yaël Powell, were brought to me at just the right time in my life and served as validation of what my Twin Flame and I had discovered on our own, without any outside influence. I can speak personally on the validity of this Twin Flame relationship as I was blessed enough in my lifetime to have been with my Twin Flame. Our story is for another time and another place, but it is important to state without qualification that the reality of the soulmate bond as expressed through God's Messages is not a fabrication or an idealistic view of what love can be... It is the greatest love that can be, the love of our Creator to us, and the ability to experience that kind of love within our soulmate bond." Rev. Adelle Tilton, The Church of Interfaith Christians, NE

DEDICATION

This book is dedicated to God who has guided us so perfectly in the unfolding of our SoulMate relationship.

We also dedicate this book to the awakening of humanity with our prayer that every person will open to the wondrous possibilities of the SoulMate relationship.

This book is also dedicated to Shanna, whose very presence in our life is a message from God affirming who we are together and catalyzing these messages into print.

SAY 'YES' TO LOVE,
GOD EXPLAINS SOULMATES
New Expanded Second Edition

TABLE OF CONTENTS

Introduction 1

The SoulMate Dispensation 9

THE MESSAGES FROM GOD 15

God's Assurance. The SoulMate Path and
its Importance to Humanity (June 2001) 17

How the SoulMate Manifests (September 2001) 21

It Is Giving, Not Receiving, That Reveals
the SoulMate (December 2000) 31

If Love Has Hurt You, It Was Not Real Love
(February 2000) 43

The Longing for Love Is a Spiritual Call
(September 2000) 47

The Definition of a SoulMate (September 2000) 59

Only When Finding/Being the SoulMate
Is the Priority, Will Everything Fall into Place
(September 2000) 69

Our SoulMate Is How We Can Experience God,
Without Losing Our Individuality (August 2000) 79

Give Yourself Completely to Love (August 2000) 89

Rush Headlong into Love (September 2000) 97

The Path of the Heart (September 2000) 103

The Truth of Love in the New Millennium
(January 2000) 113

Living in Abundance (January 2000) 121

The Question of Feeling One's Feelings
(September 2000) 129

True SoulMate Love Is Your Destiny
(November 2001) 137

ACKNOWLEDGEMENTS

I would especially like to acknowledge two women who were great spiritual lights in my life. First is Suzanne Muller who was my first teacher and the woman who ordained me. In the seven years I studied with her, she opened my eyes to the entire spectrum of spiritual belief and set my feet firmly on the spiritual path. Thirty years ago she taught me to meditate, thus establishing in my life the spiritual practice which has ultimately brought the gift of these messages.

I also want to acknowledge Bernadine Greer. Bernadine was the most generous and most beautiful light I have ever known. Bernadine was in my life in the early years of coping with such disability that I could barely move. She would sit with me by my bed for hours, bathing me in Love and most especially giving me hope. It was in one of her readings that I first heard that I would be bringing forth something, spiritually, to bless and refresh the world. Bernadine is no longer on the physical plane. I think of her often and sometimes feel her presence. It is with glad heart that I picture her watching over me.

I give thanks to Leslie Oelsner, and her husband, Geoff. Leslie has been the greatest friend a woman could have. She and Geoff have supported me with Love and light for the last eighteen years.

I also acknowledge Jim and Lorraine May, truest of friends, always ready to share the spiritual journey as well as the personal one. A Native American medicine man (ever the coyote), Jim is both trickster and big brother. Lorraine has the gentle spirit of the true Divine Feminine. Their dedication has always been an inspiration.

And to my soul sister, Michelle, who is more important to me than words can express, though our physical paths rarely cross.

To Paula, Selena and Aric for their typing, and to all the people who have touched my life and brought me growth, I give thanks. There is no way to acknowledge everyone, except to say please know that you are in my heart.

To Mary, whose life totally belongs to God, who has typed and is still typing the Messages with dedication and with Love; to her SoulMate, Steve and to her son, Michael. Michael is the first young person I have known who was raised completely conscious of spiritual reality and he is amazing!

To everyone who has touched my life I give thanks!

Yaël

Although sometimes it seems we are doing this all alone, at other times there is help there at every turn. Those people, of course, are far too numerous to mention. But there have been some amazing role models in my life.

First and foremost are my parents, Art and Betty Powell. After almost 60 years of marriage, they are still in Love and so very supportive of each other. True SoulMates!

My three brothers and sister are all also in loving relationships. Some of them have raised families and some of them are now grandparents. All of them are dedicated partners.

I also would like to acknowledge the Eureka Springs Mens' Council. For twelve years and counting they have been there for me and for each other, through everything.

My mentor, Coach Molly Seeligson, has probably been the most significant influence during my transition phase. She assisted me as I moved from an entrepreneur, a businessman, a workaholic to a truly dedicated SoulMate and husband. It was difficult for me to let go of who I thought I was so that I could become who I was meant to be.

To everyone else, I thank you and bless you for the role you have played in assisting me to grow into who I have become.

Peace,

Doug

PREFACE

Have you ever felt that an Invisible Hand was guiding your life? Well, that Hand brought me to the Messages you are about to read – but by a very long and circuitous route. May I share a little of the story?

In the early 1980's, music was my profession. I had been Administrative Director of a professional chamber orchestra and then became Chairperson of the Music Division at the College of Santa Fe (NM) for five years. During this time I was also given an additional assignment — to develop a new non-traditional program for adults returning to college. As I interviewed people for this program, people whose pathway no longer satisfied their life needs, I came to realize that *I was one of them!* Something powerful was compelling me, too, to make a major change.

I became a student once again and completed a Masters degree in Counseling. Life took some unexpected turns before the change fully materialized but eventually I found my special place as an elementary public school counselor in Maine and then North Carolina. The past eleven years in this profession have given me a deep appreciation of the beauty and perfection of each person's unfoldment. Giving myself unconditionally to these beautiful little children quietly healed my own painful childhood.

While this was my outer world, my inner world was all about spirituality and metaphysics. How can one walk on Planet Earth today without asking what life here is all about? My personal path led me to hundreds of books, an important teacher, many self-healing modalities and workshops, devoted meditation and prayer, and most important, constant examination and questioning. I had always had a persistent feeling deep within that there was a spiritual task for me with which I had not yet connected. All of my prayers had not brought the answer. This was a source of great frustration to me.

2001 found me feeling overwhelming restlessness. I had recently changed schools but the challenge of the new setting had not subdued an inner compulsion toward I knew not what. The Invisible Hand again intervened and led me to an astrologer, Julian Lee, who specializes in finding the best geographical location for people. I had studied astrology and had respect for this tool. Julian's information showed that Northwest Arkansas was the optimal region for the unfolding of my life in the coming decade. Nothing could have surprised me more. I had never been to Arkansas and would never have envisioned the Ozarks as my future home.

On July 17, the date suggested as propitious, I flew to Fayetteville, Arkansas on an exploratory trip. I felt a mixture of adventure, trepidation and courage and determination. I had no idea what I was going to find. My only resources were a couple of names and a free place to stay, thanks to a friend of a friend. Upon arrival at the home of my hostess, I was invited to join a party revolving around a unique couple, Yaël and Doug Powell. The most magnetic thing about Yaël and Doug was their obvious living love for each other that pervaded their every word and movement. I was fascinated. I learned that Yaël lives housebound, in constant pain from a genetic disease of the spine that severely limits her movement. They had only traveled from their home in Eureka Springs to Fayetteville – a rare excursion – this particular evening because it was Yaël's birthday.

Following dinner Yaël read one of the "Messages from God" that have come through her during thirty years of daily meditation. I felt incredible excitement and upliftment from the extraordinary vibration created and the amazing information of this Message. The topic was SoulMates. That Message is in this book.

I made a date to meet with them at their home in Eureka Springs on Beaver Lake. There they have created a beautiful Light Center, Circle of Light, that includes the Wedding Chapel that is their business and service. We spent two bliss filled days together, reconnecting, sharing our lives, our spiritual journeys and recognizing ourselves as the ancient Soul Family we are. I have never felt greater love. Our coming together was divinely guided, step by step. Yaël showed me fifty hand-written notebooks of Messages from God! I had at last found my special task. I committed myself on the spot to helping them bring this illuminated and needed material out into the world. Christmas of 2001 found me in my new home at Circle of Light Spiritual Center.

And the Messages? Each day Yaël surrenders herself to God in meditation and sometimes hand-writes as many as 25 pages of exquisite guidance to humanity. Much of this speaks of the importance of the SoulMate relationship, heretofore not understood on the planet. The Messages also often guide each of us personally and give us specific tasks. It was an October 2001 Message (before I moved to Circle of Light) that urged us to get the first book out to the world as quickly as possible. A tremendous surge of teamwork followed by phone, fax and email, and you have the second edition of that book in your hands.

Yaël and Doug have surmounted many physical and emotional adversities, both individually and in their relationship during their fourteen-year marriage. Their purity and faith shine forth, and the feeling from the words they bring forth is undeniable. They hold in their hands a rare Beacon of Light for a confused world. As God has told them, "My call to humanity is embedded in these Messages. Beloved ones, if this relationship between us is clear and true, others will know…they will feel My Presence. My Love does 'ride upon your words.' I am writing to the world through you."

I invite you to open your heart and enter a world where Love is all there is, a world of beauty, of peace and hope, and above all, of connection to your SoulMate through the Messages from God.

Shanna Mac Lean
Eureka Springs, AR
March 2003

INTRODUCTION

It was December of 1986, the Winter Solstice. Doug and I had just married. We sat together to meditate—a practice I had been faithfully doing at that time for fifteen years, a practice that had fed me and sustained me through the death of my son and through the loss of physical mobility to a powerful genetic disease.

Two years earlier I had begun to receive Messages. They began at the time I lost my mobility. I was in great physical and emotional pain. I was very seriously considering ending my life. Through this dark night God reached forth with an incredible Love and gave me the strength to continue. There was no doubt about who it was lifting me and renewing my faith in life. The Messages then were "flashes" of Love and of light. I would be wrapped in God's Divine Presence. I would be given an "instant understanding" of some part of me that needed illumination. It was like receiving a "package" that was a totality—all the Love and all the information—-all at once "dropped" into my head. At that time I recorded these experiences in a form that was like poetry. The understandings were like beacons and the Love sustained me as I gathered the fortitude to re-connect to life.

Now, on this December day I sat for the first time with Doug, my new husband and the Love of my life. Although we had many a rocky road to travel ahead of us, even then we knew we were each other's destiny. I

1

closed my eyes and touched Doug's hand. My entire being exploded into light — a loving, pulsing light that was alive with movement and luminosity. Dancing golden white particles shone all around me, joining together into a greater and greater light. The sense of loving presence grew, filled my heart and poured through me. My heart caught on fire. There is no other way to describe it. The fire leaped the gap between Doug and me and drew us together into an experience of becoming living flames ourselves, dancing together, "burning" in love and reaching higher and higher.

In the midst of this experience I knew I had to write. I reached for a notebook and pen. As I wrote I was aware of being assisted with the energy, but though illuminated by God's Love, it was my words that I was using, doing my best to describe what is indescribable.

Thus these Messages began. They have now lovingly, unfailingly guided us through fifteen years of marriage. They have kept us going when we were ready to give up. They have explained ourselves to us. They have revealed to us our destiny – that step-by-step, we were to clear the way so others could make this journey quickly — the one that took us all these years.

God has taken us through every phase of our relationship. We have lived through the experience of ego, and we have been guided to an ever-greater knowing that we could choose our hearts. When our egos had us run and hide, God showed us how to choose to Love. When we found ourselves immobilized by our fear, God carefully returned us to the truth that we are ever held in grace. When it seemed we began to live separate lives, God showed us choices we had to make that brought back our ability to see our hearts again. And God showed us how each moment's choice was ours, and day-by-day helped us make sure our choice was Love and nothing else.

God revealed to us our destiny — not an instant perfect Love, but instead, a gradual awareness of how our deep truth as SoulMates could be reclaimed as we learned to say "yes" to Love ever more deeply. It is a destiny in which we have walked each step so we could be ready to serve you in your awakening to your SoulMate and to the power of your Love.

We have not "had it easy," but where we have come is more beautiful than anything we could have ever dreamed for ourselves! As we have grown together as a result of God's tender guiding Love, we have also grown in our ability to open ourselves, to rise up to meet God at a higher level. We have grown in our ability to experience our glorious SoulMate union, and in doing so, we have been greatly blessed with understanding of the "piece" of information that is our destiny to share – the beautiful truth about SoulMates.

We want to tell you that everything you've ever dreamed is true! True Love is your destiny and the Love you will share with your SoulMate will be so magnificent, so glorious, so beautiful, so tender and so filled with ecstasy that no words can even begin to tell the joy of the experience. Don't stop believing! Don't let anything dissuade you, especially not your previous experiences and definitely not the normal definitions of relationship.

Instead, place everything, all of your energy and your trust, in the knowledge that God is so filled with Love for us that we are each created with a SoulMate. Know that wherever we are, God's Love will be real, embodied forever right in front of us in our SoulMate or Twin Flame. Keep affirming it. Keep choosing Love. Keep looking for your SoulMate with your heart and not your ego, and we promise you will find him or her. The biggest surprise might be for you as it has for us – that he or she is right in front of you. You've just forgotten how to see with your heart.

Know that God will now take you with tender care on this journey to your SoulMate. These Messages are far more than simply words. Every word is filled with Love, with packages of light, to be delivered to any who are open as they read. So please say "yes!" to Love, as God requests. Then you, as with us, will be filled with gratitude every single moment.

Where God has taken us through these Messages is like a fairy tale. Had we not lived it, it would be hard to believe, but we have lived it. Our life together has unfolded into more and more and more light, and Love and beauty. We have been given the greatest gift two human beings can receive — the gift of being SoulMates. We have been given the gift of being more and more in Love, every moment of every day. We have had the gift of watching our hearts join and our energies blossom, and the gift of seeing how this experience that God is leading us through is a spiritual experience and a spiritual path of breathtaking beauty.

We are still learning. We are learning that this gift is now available to absolutely every human being; that it is a part of the awakening that is upon us. We are learning how the shared heart is a chamber for manifestation; and we are learning how to live each and every moment from the level of the heart.

As we look around us we can see the Love and beauty coming into view in every area of our lives. We want, more than anything else, to share this blessing with others.

So with the deepest gratitude and humility, we offer God's Messages on SoulMates. We are very aware of our limitation as we strive to find words to describe the experience of communion with God, an experience that is absolutely beyond the capacity of our mind. So please do not allow the words to limit your experience of the Messages, including our use of the word " God" to describe this most magnificent One, the vast Love that is personal yet limitless. Instead, please read with your heart, allowing the packages of Love and truth held behind each word to come forth to you. We know we have received these Messages through our hearts for they represent a very real and personal relationship with God – a relationship that continually transforms our life and the lives of other who read the Messages.

As we offer these Messages to you, we ask that you simply open your heart as wide as you can, and reach upward to your highest vision. Allow the energy of these Messages to verify their source and to bring their blessings into your life. We humbly offer our experience: that even the Messages we could not understand nonetheless blessed us and moved us into greater awareness.

By now it is obvious that a great "uprising" of Love is in progress in our world. All who are truly dedicated to the Light will be vessels for God's Love, to pour that Love forth in our unique ways.

We ask that, as you read God's Messages, if your heart verifies their truth to you, that you speak the words that are the key to the embodiment of Love for our times: "I want my SoulMate." Then, hang on for the ride as your heart opens and Love is revealed, intimately, to you. To this end, we offer you our assistance, as the coming of Love for this age takes shape in your life.

Yaël & Doug
Circle of Light
Eureka Springs, AR
April 2003

THE SOULMATE DISPENSATION

The SoulMate dispensation is a magnificent gift from God to humanity. It is also a significant factor in the awakening of humanity to Love.

As God has explained to us through the Messages, there is a universal law of resonance which operates unfailingly throughout Creation. Simply stated, it is the truth about vibration – that like vibration attracts like vibration. Thus, whatever our vibrational "sum," that is what we attract into our lives.

In our evolution, we would not draw our SoulMate, our glorious Twin Flame, the reflection of our perfection in Love, until we were just that – perfected. This means there would be more growth and evolution for most of us before we could possibly hope to make that connection. Most would not connect with their SoulMate until "beyond the veil," when no longer living a life in the world.

The SoulMate dispensation is a special dispensation by God that allows our SoulMate to come to us now, before we are perfected enough to draw him or her through the natural process of resonance. This means that all on Earth now have access to their

SoulMate, their one Twin Flame, right where they are in their path of awakening, regardless of whether or not their resonance is only Love.

What this does is allow true Love to now be made manifest in every person's life. The reason for this dispensation is that once this Love is experienced, this Love will then open each person's heart. It will be the proof that Love exists and that God loves each of us so much that the proof of Love is always embodied in our life.

The only time that most people touch the truth of Love and really experience life with the heart is when they fall in Love. So, this special gift from God of having access to our SoulMate means that couple after couple will be returned to this experience of joy, of life fresh and beautiful that happens when one falls in Love. Because of this, people will remember what it feels like to live in Love as God intended rather than fear which is the result of the ego's desire for separation and its fear of Love.

Most importantly, the Love that is generated by an awakened SoulMate couple is more powerful than we can yet imagine. It has the capacity to lift the world, to open hearts and to send forth great waves of Love that will unfreeze the frozen places in the hearts of humanity. God has said that it will not take many truly open, reunited SoulMates to completely shift this world to only Love and thus to free us all from duality and ego.

It does not matter if you understand what all of

this means. It only matters that you put out the call in your heart for your SoulMate — that you say "yes" each day to the opening of your heart to Love. What matters is that you know that the longing for Love you've always felt was placed there by God. It's meant to keep you looking for your SoulMate, so you can live in Love, together, in the world.

You will discover some amazing things as you allow the longing for your SoulMate to return. You'll discover that in pushing away the belief in perfect Love, you have pushed away a very real part of yourself. You've pushed away the route for your return to who you really are. One heart with two flames, One Love with two parts.

As you allow God to lead you through these Messages, you will come to an ever-deeper appreciation of the magnificent gift God has given us through the SoulMate dispensation. Not only will it give every single person the Love they have been waiting for. It will give humanity back the truth that we are only Love and nothing else.

Do you remember falling in Love? Do you remember the feeling of joy? The ecstasy? The sense that you were wrapped in someone's Love? That you could see things and feel things as never before?

If you can remember those feelings, then I invite you to feel them again, right now. You are meant to live that way – and more. You are meant to live each day totally "head-over-heels in Love." Every moment should be a glory because your Love is alive in the world. Colors should be brighter, the touch of material objects more sensuous. That magical feeling of expectancy is your gift to use as the continual attraction of more and more good. More good, more Love.

When two people fall in Love, for a time the whole world changes. Things do look different, and they have different meaning.

What is happening in things like this? Here is the important answer. ***When people fall in Love, they access the world through their heart! They are seeing the world as it really is for the first time.***

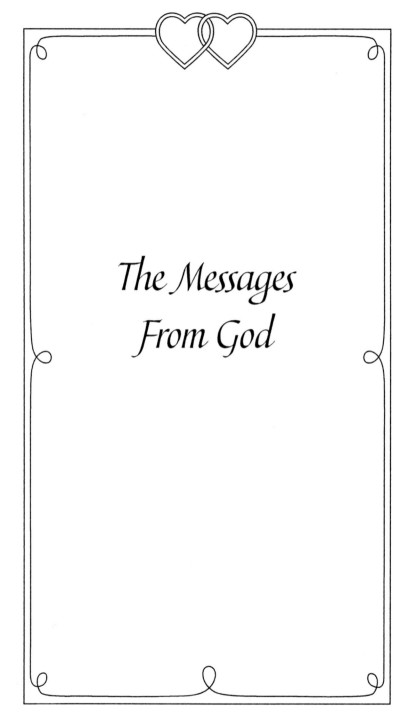

The Messages
From God

You are meant to
breathe My name with every breath!
To speak My Love
with every sentence.
To worship in joy at the altar
of our communion.
Permanently.

God's Assurance.
The SoulMate Path
and Its Importance to Humanity

My dear ones, in the Messages that follow I am giving to you one of the keys to heaven. I am sharing with you the path to ascension for the whole of humanity. Please do not doubt this. *I promise you that the SoulMate relationship is not only real. It is the way for humankind to grow into their divinity.*

How many people do you know who are making the effort to live their spirituality? How many of these same people are confused or lack structure or motivation? How many of their lives are caught up in the world? The answer to this question is: most of those who love Me, those you would consider the "highest" people around you.

Many people speak of "loving humanity" but one of the pitfalls of this idea is that it is easy to never truly open one's heart. A person can call himself altruistic or spiritual while never having to crack the protective shell.

To open to your SoulMate is to truly open your heart, to allow Love to come before you and live with you, face-to-face. To open to your SoulMate is to ask yourself every moment — is my heart open? Am I willing to choose Love? to believe in my heart? Am I willing to "walk my talk"? If you are, Love will manifest. "As above, so below." If your heart is open, your SoulMate will appear.

There will be some who do not like to hear this. It is because their hearts are blocked for whatever reason, but they do not want to believe it. But as in all things, dear ones, **what is manifesting in a person's life is "the inside coming out."** As within, so without. What is within will show up in front of you. It will manifest and be mirrored exactly in the form of relationship. People must acknowledge this. They must get "up close and personal" in order to truly move through "the gate."

Now, once together, it is imperative that the SoulMate couple turns outward and gives. Only so will my Love be fully received, fully incarnated.

Humankind is now on the edge of comprehending manifestation. At present they are just barely acknowledging it. The SoulMate relationship is a part of the whole truth of manifestation. If you are still in your ego, it is very difficult to admit to your limitations, your blocks, and the areas where you do not allow Love. Yet, real spiritual growth requires full responsibility.

Thus, if abundance is not manifesting physically in your life, you must examine this. You must be ruthlessly honest. The ego will keep people hopping from one relationship to another and will sabotage any real Love, because true Love is the elimination of ego and the opening of the heart. *The heart knows that when it is open, your SoulMate is there. The more open the heart, the more fully the SoulMate can come into view.*

Normally as a being ascends in vibration, the connection to the SoulMate naturally occurs as an "out of body" experience, because the higher level allows one to see the truth more easily. But now, humanity must collectively open the heart. There is no better way than through conscious commitment to manifesting the SoulMate relationship. As you work together to embody the SoulMate union, you will become intimately acquainted with your own capacity to love and you will also experience My Love as it is manifesting before you and within you.

There are many ways that people can choose to reach the level of Love needed for the transformation of humanity and the Earth. The SoulMate experience is the direct path. It is Love, focusing on Love, opening to Love, living in Love!

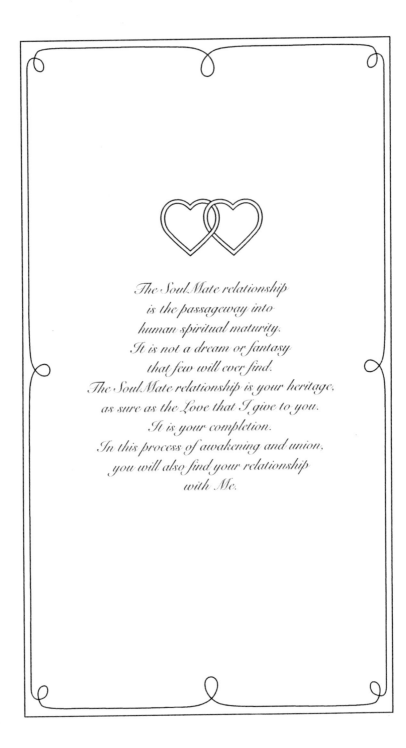

The Soul Mate relationship
is the passageway into
human spiritual maturity.
It is not a dream or fantasy
that few will ever find.
The Soul Mate relationship is your heritage,
as sure as the Love that I give to you.
It is your completion.
In this process of awakening and union,
you will also find your relationship
with Me.

How the SoulMate Manifests

Dear ones, I am here. I rock you in a cradle of stars as you discover that you are vast and full of beauty. I help you see your place in the grand design, and I whisper to you that just as surely as those stars maintain their course, just that surely will I guide you. As surely as the cycles of the Earth bring the seasons, as surely as such movements hold the messages of your connection to all things, so do I place your hands together with your SoulMate's, with whom you will experience Love never ending and in whom you can always know yourself.

I ask you to remember this deeper conversation in all things in every moment. In all the eons of your development, the two of you, the halves of the whole that is the cell of My heart, have been many things. You have danced together into the world; you have danced separately at times. Yet no matter where you have been at any time, you have always shared your energy. You have known that your SoulMate was alive, real and with you, because you have never left each other.

If indeed Creation is holographic, it means that there are always two ways you can do everything. You can do it through the many layers of Creation, through worlds and vibrations, through bodies, through lifetimes, in and out of awareness of each other. Or you can do it directly by understanding that in a hologram everything is fully present in every other thing. This means, dear ones, that *you and your SoulMate, though seemingly separated, really are not.* If you realize this truth, you can go right through to him or her. You can realize that they are always with you. They are in you and you are in them. This is always the truth, just as I am here fully present within everything.

Listen. *It is the same here on Earth as it is when you dream.* You are involved in a long, drawn-out moment just as when you dream. So your mind is busy weaving through the illusion of Time, back and forth, threading the lines of your life through the artificial structure of Time. Yet it seems very real to you. You are dreaming that you are not with your SoulMate. It is not true. Yet what you are dreaming is what you need to learn. It is fabricated by the need for growth, for revelation.

Now, believe it or not, from the level of truth, you are here busily talking to yourself. Oh, I know it does not seem this way. But neither does a dream feel like a dream when you are dreaming. It feels very real. You are scared or you are happy. You are with many different people. Some are your lovers; others are your enemies. Yet when you wake, you realize that every one of them is really a part of you. So if you are available for personal growth, you examine the dream to see what it teaches you.

Dear ones, this is the truth about your life here as well. From within the dream it feels so real, yet in truth you are a vast being, huge beyond your imagining, keeper of stars within your belly, worlds within your brain. And whole civilizations are alive to love because they exist in your heart. You are such beings, for you are made in My image and I Am All That Is.

You are dreaming that you are limited beings living a limited life. You are dreaming this for what it will teach you about creating with Me. You are dreaming this so you will understand compassion, humility, repression, limitation, and the power of both Love and consciousness.

You ask how I could tell you that you can awaken your heart and choose your SoulMate, and your SoulMate will be there with you. This makes you struggle to comprehend what I am saying. You are ready now to understand. You can jump high enough to see past the illusion you are living.

In truth, all relationships in your life are energy agreements. They are energy agreements made with other vast, huge, glorious beings like you. They are energy agreements that say, "while we are asleep, I need to learn about compassion. You need to learn about limitation. What do you say that we go to sleep and dream that I am a mother and you are my disabled, disfigured child?" You would say, "Oh, that is perfect; let's do so now!" Then you both go to sleep and in your dreams you meet as mother and child.

Now, you are vast beings, holders of universes, sleeping and dreaming lots of dreams simultaneously, because of course there is not really any Time. That, too, is part of the dream. So before you go to sleep you are aware that part of your lesson is to learn lucid dreaming – to understand you are dreaming as you are doing so. You are also aware that you are planning an evolutionary lucid dream together.

So here you are in your dream. You get to the point where you begin your lucid dreaming. You are remembering who you are. At this point you say the "code words" you have given yourself. You say, "I want to see my SoulMate." And you begin to shift your perception from the one in the dream to the one who is dreaming. At this point, the other dreamers, whose energies have been in your dream in the character of your husband or wife or girlfriend or boyfriend, are withdrawn. It's no problem – it's only a dream anyway – and that dreamer has many more dreams going on.

Your SoulMate comes in. Your SoulMate is real, another vast and glorious part of the wholeness that is the two of you. Your SoulMate must still at this point come to you in the dream, so your SoulMate will use whatever image is already in the dream with you.

But because you are now beginning the lucid dreaming, you are involved in the dream as who you are. You are beginning to recognize the nature of true Reality. It is the fastest way to awakening to rejoin with your SoulMate because your SoulMate can show your true self to you perfectly (you are, after all, two parts of the same being). You know you are accomplishing the lucid dream because whoever was in front of you, you now recognize as your SoulMate. You can feel their energy. You can sense the truth of their Love and the depth of their knowledge of you. So all that went before in that earlier part of the dream shifts easily, as dreams do, and you are there with your SoulMate.

Where did the "other person" go? The other person was also a dream figment created by the two of you to fill your need for growth. (Don't shift back to your other smaller perspective here!) Your SoulMate is always there with you – always. You are sleeping beside each other wrapped in each other's arms. So the whole time you have been dreaming, your SoulMate has been holding you, loving you, filling you with his or her energy and scent. Your heartbeats are mingled. You are so close that even your dreams are not your own. Your SoulMate is there with you every moment, wrapped around and within the dream, helping you plot out what you need to learn before you can share the lucid dream. And then, from the lucid dream, you will begin to awaken together.

Your SoulMate has been with you through every relationship. If you open to it, you will remember his or her energy. Together you are sharing your lives while having seemingly separate dreams. But they are not really separate. There is much of your SoulMate's energy always around you, and there are also "fingers" of other beings' energies as you teach each other in your dreams. As your real selves, you always know how close you are to remembering the lucid dreaming, and your energy combinations shift accordingly, assisted of course by the beautiful angels and guides who are helping you. They make sure that the right mix of energies is always present and that every dream adventure leads you closer to the recognition.

This is one of the reasons why I have said that your SoulMate is a shortcut to fully awakening. Not only can your SoulMate reflect to you your true self; he or she also can help you to remember who you are. Quickly.

Dear ones, you are glorious beings dreaming together in a beautiful slumber. Vast beings. Each of you has "fingers of light" extending down into the "sleeping world" — fingers of consciousness, dream selves dreaming in every time period and in every character. This is why I have said to you before that Reality is much more fluid than you would think! Remember what you know of "life after death?" Remember how in the "heaven world" people simply manifest what they want around them and with whom? It's the same here in your life at this level. You are just vibrating slowly enough that your manifestations appear to happen through Time. Thus, as you choose to have your experience be one with your SoulMate and you open your heart, you begin to perceive with the heart, and thus to see the world truly.

Please share this news. All who begin the lucid dreaming will be awakening ever more fully into the Reality behind the dream. I can assure you *it is not a matter of "finding" your SoulMate. It is a matter of opening to seeing your SoulMate.*

So as you no longer need or want the lessons you

have been choosing to learn, your heart can call in the experience of your SoulMate. It is not as if the person you were with then has to leave. Rather, the energy mix enlivening that being simply and elegantly changes. More of your SoulMate's energy is there, and the energy of the "character" of the other being's dream becomes less and less and less, until it is fully the energy of your SoulMate enlivening the being before you. The energy of the other being will either join another dream in progress or will be reabsorbed by the Sleeping Giant of Love that was invested in your dream to learn with you. In this particular time of awakening, hopefully that "finger of light" will go join with the dream in which that being is awakening to his or her SoulMate.

Reality is consciousness. It is Love molded by Will. It is only and always that energy. And the entire goal is the awareness of Love. *So in your lives, my beautiful ones, you may trust that your choice to love fully from your heart and to invest in your SoulMate will mean that your SoulMate will be standing before you.* He or she may appear clothed perhaps, conveniently, in the current imagery, but feeling completely different. As you open your heart more and more fully, you are elevating your consciousness beyond the dream. You begin seeing Love, and seeing Love means seeing your SoulMate. Seeing your SoulMate means knowing yourself, knowing yourself as Love, in Love, being Love, which means knowing Me. Knowing Me means awakening beyond the need for dreaming and into the shared co-creation. *You the dreamers awake, and take your places in the fully conscious universe. All of you together are the emissary of My heart.*

Thus, just as a physical heart nourishes all parts of a physical vehicle, so you together, who are part of My heart, nourish My body which holds all things within it.

Please do not worry if you cannot grasp this. Just look for your SoulMate in your partner's eyes and you will recognize them even if you could have sworn he/she was not there before. Trust Me on this and I will show you the awakening of the heart in every sense, including the re-union with your SoulMate. Trust this and you will be given proof as your life turns into what your heart has longed for. You will not care about the mechanics of how it got there. You will be too busy being Love. All you have to do is trust Me enough to say "yes" to love, and to make the choice to truly open your heart. The only thing you have to do is move beyond your ego in order to recognize your truth in Love. Once done you will have your proof, as you become aware of the perfection of the dream and the glory of the truth within it.

Remember the hologram.

You must expand
the Love within you
until it manifests the Love without
so clearly
that you live every moment
in absolute surety
of this reality of Love.

It Is Giving, Not Receiving, that Reveals the SoulMate

The gift of light comes to wash you and lift you so that every cell within you is joining in the dance of light that is Creation. Glowing, sparkling, whirling, touching, being touched, lifting and being lifted.

It is the season of light, where the illumination of humankind began, where the veil opens and the Christ light enters easily. Now I reach forth and I light you and you, and you. You are now the candles in the window of the world. You in turn must light those who come to you, until all the world is illuminated and truth is revealed in everything.

There is a secret to this illumination that it is time to discover. It is the secret of union. It is the path of the SoulMate. With illumination comes the communion of Love.

All of Creation is My giving. It is the movement of My Love as it pours forth with so much energy, so much passion, so much joy that out of this movement universes are born, worlds come whirling into being. Call it a "Big Bang" if you like, but the beginning of All That Is was My overwhelming need to give forth, to share My Love, to pour Myself into life, to expand My being through giving My Love. This is the "out-breath of God," the active spark from which all is born. Thus, it is My nature to give.

It is this energy of giving that is the foundation of life, and as you are made in My image, it is your nature also. But more than being your nature, you must understand that *giving is the divine energy of Creation and the basis for everything.*

When I understood My need to share this universe that came into existence from My desire to give, that became "the in-breath of God." That was the moment when I turned My Creation so that Creation could also see Me. Giving forth, turning and finding deeper awareness in seeing and being seen. Deep in My being I understood at that moment in Creation that I needed an intelligence — a consciousness with which to share the awareness of the entirety of My being and thus of Creation. So, from the Love of My heart you were made.

In your being, all of the principles of Creation exist, and the consciousness to share the awareness of all of Creation. Now you have developed your individuality, and it becomes time to claim that consciousness. I will show you all that is within you. Every beauty is within you. Every spark of life, every capacity for Love. Built into your very beings on every level is the essential flow of the energy of life. You have found it in your genes. You have discovered it in your consciousness. Now, you will find it in your fullness, which is your awakening with your SoulMate.

Why do I not say it is in "finding" your SoulMate? Why do I say "awakening"? Because your SoulMate is never apart from you. It is impossible for you to be separated. Dear ones, in truth you are one being. *You are one being, temporarily unable to see the other part of yourselves even though that part is right in front of you.*

How can this be? How can I say such a thing when whole lives are given to the search for this SoulMate? How can I expect you to believe such a thing, when people live alone and die, all the while wishing for that SoulMate? I know it will be difficult to believe at first but over time you will come to understand this truth. *You are separated by vibrational disparity – the inability of the "apparatus" of the physical vehicle to be aware of the subtle world around you.*

This disparity is changing. It is being eliminated as the physical apparatus becomes less physical. As the individuation is accomplished, then each of your evolutions turns back toward Me, and just as with the larger Creation, you become able to see your own creations, your own world and the parts of yourselves. Why? Because now rather than looking outward only as the expanding creation, you are also looking back at Me as the returning creation.

You and your SoulMate are one being. Between you, you contain every energy of Creation. You exemplify every law of Creation. You are a "packet" of all that is! You are the crown of Creation, My glory, the pinnacle of My Love. You are that which exemplifies everything that is in Me. And together, the energy flow between you reflects the pattern of the creative energy in everything.

There is a reason that this is coming forward now in December 2000 on the cusp of the millennium of awakening. All are now opening their hearts to the level of Love that is. Eternity will experience the embodiment of this Love which is the SoulMate union. The truth, the embodiment of My Love is the two of you together as one.

As "the smoke clears" – the "smoke" being the thick nature of lower vibrational reality — you will become aware of your SoulMate. Then, as you turn homeward, you will begin to understand the flow of energy between you. From the larger perspective, the coming together of these SoulMate unions will be the connecting of the vibrational level of Reality with that of this world. Yes, like "clicking" into place, when each SoulMate couple comes together, that couple will become an anchor or a channel for what you call The Christ. In truth this means becoming the full embodiment of My Love.

Those of you who know that your SoulMate is before you (or even if you suspect) must begin to work with the flow of Love and the flow of energy between you, for you can quickly raise the level of your energy and begin to see "above the fog." Oh, My children, how much Love is waiting for you! How much joy! How much fulfillment! And how much you will bring to the transformation of humanity, of the Earth.

I ask you all then to put away every fear of Love, to let go of everything that you believe impedes this deep and holy partnership. I tell you that if you make this your "spiritual path," the focus of your awakening, everything will fall in place. I do understand how powerfully the ego wants to cling to all its carefully constructed illusions of separateness. And I tell you that these illusions are lies. *Your heart knows the truth. The truth is that every human heart has been searching for its SoulMate. Every one, because this is how you are made.*

You are two energies of one being, and the flow of energy between you is the exact pattern of the flow of energy through all Creation. It is what I have called the double helix of Creation so you will understand the importance of this information. It is life flowing between you. Directed by the consciousness and fueled by your Love, it can become anything you want it to.

The most important information for you is that *the motion of energy that fuels this double helix is GIVING. It is NOT receiving.* Once you understand this, you hold the key in your hands to your awakening and to truth. The most important energy of Creation is GIVING. It fuels everything. It is the beginning. It is the "Big Bang" and all the "little bangs" that follow (humor). You cannot get or keep the energy flowing between SoulMates without this. The energy of giving is nourishment to everything.

In the human body there is a constant flow of energy up the spine. On the most physical level this is the cerebral-spinal fluid. In the SoulMate, there is also a flow of energy that provides life to the whole. It follows the path of the double helix. It flows from chakra to chakra, wrapping around, traveling the spine (the kundalini) and coming back down.

At every chakra the SoulMate energy from the two people is exchanged. It goes in one person, up and out to the other. To function on the level of Reality, this energy must constantly stay flowing. It is kept in motion by giving.

By the sending forth of Love at each "joining" (each chakra), the SoulMate couple has an opening to whatever level of energy that chakra represents. Through that opening they serve the world at that level. The more consciously the energy is given forth, the more powerfully it affects things around it. *It is imperative that a SoulMate couple gives together of the energy and Love they possess.* Ideally (when evolved), the light will pour out of each and every chakra where the two are joined. This pulls the highest energy of Creation into their system and then gives it outward to humankind/Earth or wherever it is directed.

It is these "activated" SoulMate unions that can and will instantly uplift this world and all that is connected to it. There are many ways for a SoulMate couple to connect with and direct energy. One of the most powerful is sexual union. Of course I will tell you more about this.* For now though, let Me say that sexual union is the most potent creative force in the world. It is meant to be used by human beings to fuel the power of creation you possess. On any level it is a creative force. What is held in the mind and heart during sexual union is sent forth into existence. This is why sexual union has such magnetism for human beings. It is also the creative energy behind many human hells as well as many heavens.

I do understand that some of this information may sound "out there" to some. Others will recognize it instantly. Many of you who have remembered the truth in this life on Earth will say that you have always known this about sexual union. Many more will remember even at a very young age being sure they were waiting for their SoulMate.

You have often heard "when the pupil is ready, the teacher appears." Know also that when the heart is open, the SoulMate becomes visible, very likely in the person you are with. It will be true as long as that person can open his/her heart. That is all it takes to allow the SoulMate to become embodied in you. *It is the energy of giving that will begin the movement of SoulMate energy between two people.* Thus, do not judge someone's ability to open his/her heart until you are able to give, cleanly, clearly, of the Love of your own heart, for most of the time when you do, the person before you will awaken.

Many people go searching for their SoulMate, waiting for someone to give so much to them that they will recognize their SoulMate. Now you can see this is the incorrect approach! The only way to see your SoulMate is to get the energy of the double helix of life working between you. The only way it can be started is through giving. So it is true you could find someone who already understood this and would give to you on the level of the heart or above, but why wait? And do not be deceived by the ego! *Oh, the ego will do anything to convince you that you are giving when you are not!* Giving from the ego level is an empty show. It is not real and thus it will never connect you. Of course, this is just what the ego wants, for its goal is to stay in existence.

So when you come to Me in meditation or to receive guidance, remember that at the crown of the double helix you are completely joined to Me. You then have consciousness of all the levels of truth. The crown is the level of the fully connected SoulMate human being, co-creator of the universe.

So how do you get yourself to the level you want in order to make this connection? How do you connect with the energy of Creation which is the larger double helix? By giving! So as you open your heart with your SoulMate each day, you must actively give Love to him or her. Jump start the flow! Tap into the helix. EXPAND outward, reaching to them. Move your energy. Do not sit passively waiting to receive. Once you make that connection, you will be the connection through which My Love is made manifest in the world.

What you have considered as the "sign of infinity" (it looks like a figure 8) is meant to be the helix on the current physical plane. Thus, the energy pattern of all Creation is the "sign of infinity." As you become open-hearted beings, functioning in the New World or Reality, it will become just three connections, crown, throat and heart. For now it is all of the connections. I will, in time, show you how to lift the sexual connection from the base to the heart.

Please do not let the details overwhelm you. Just let them fall, like rain – gentle rain, into your consciousness. Then as your heart opens, you will understand what is happening as you feel yourselves connecting to these energies.

Awake, My beloved children. Awake! Open your beautiful eyes on the level where you can see Me. Open your heart so you can experience My Love. And then, fueled by awareness, take your Love and speak the truth of your united being, and create. Bring into view a new addition to My Creation, a new Love to My heart and a new surprise in My consciousness. Experience life as the energy of giving and you will be blessed with awakening.

*See **Say "Yes" to Love, God Unveils SoulMate Love and Sacred Sexuality** published in 2002.

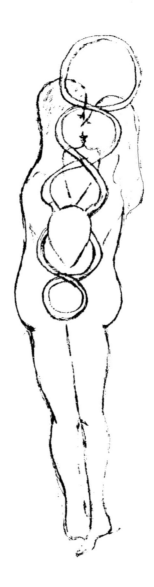

The heart must open
in order for you to transform.
To open, it must be ready to give —
to give up what it is
for the promise
of what it will become.
To do this, it must give itself to another.
The promise of Love
is worth the risk of losing what you are,
for the sake of becoming
what Love will make of you.
It is only through another
that you will know yourself.

If Love Has Hurt You, It Was Not Real Love

I am here with you every moment, like the beating of your heart, the air you breathe and the beauty you see when you look into the world. You are never away from Me. Not ever. The substance of your being is the substance of Mine.

What I want you to see, then, is that the moment you turn yourselves to open to me, I am here. Rushing in! Touching you, moving, exalting you. With every moment, every beat of your heart, all things are entrained to you. All things around you are brought into harmony with Me through you.

This is what I ask of you — that your heart be filled with Love. *Love can never harm — not even accidentally.* I will say this to you again. LOVE CAN NEVER HARM. It is the nature of Love that it always heals — heals all hearts, heals emotions and heals the mind. *If Love has ever hurt you, it was not really Love. It was the ego disguised as Love.* It was forces of separation masquerading as servers of light. Thus, when I tell you that Love cannot be damaged or betrayed, I ask that you allow this in. As you do, you will come into a real relationship with Love, and only so can we have the communion that is the grace and joy and foundation of your existence.

Can you absorb this? Please — you must. Most people have never had contact with real Love. But they believe they have. And thus they feel justified in villainizing Love and hiding from it.

When you truly live in Love, there is bliss. There is the continual awareness of overflowing joy. Real love always supports you. It always makes you more, never less.

It is because human hearts do know their birthright that the belief in Love persists. When you live in real Love, there is only the uplifting movement from joy to ever-deeper joy. Some of you are now beginning to experience real Love. You begin to see the ever-deepening respect of real Love. And the tenderness.

Once you have achieved real Love with someone, that relationship will only grow, as long as you do not turn away. So, this is the truth of Love. True Love always gives more, always loves more, always illuminates. And you can choose real Love.

Please, dear ones, please sit and absorb this. Real Love will never portray you as anything but your real self. Real Love will not ever leave you suffering. There are many theories about relationship that say that people are meant to move on, to be "serial monogamists," to "learn more and more lessons." This is not true. **Love is the highest goal. It is the one true goal.** It can be brought into being by the desire of your heart. And, if Love is real, there are no more "lessons" to learn.

If you will turn your precious hearts to Me, I will teach you how to live in Love. I will show you how Love feels, for I will fill you with My Love. As My Love pours in to you, to uplift, enfold and bless, so will you love. Love will clear away the illusions of ego and you will know that all of the pain you have experienced was never the result of Love. It was, instead, the ego masquerading as Love. Love will show you a different experience, adding joy onto joy, as its truth becomes your new experience.

Believe in Love, dear ones. Choose Love in faith and it will lead you perfectly back to the truth of who you are.

You are made
as a movement of My Love
going forth to touch Creation
through My heart.
You hold a special energy.
Your very soul is a perfect window
through which My Love is focused
in outward movement.
Thus, if each and every human being
were simply to allow
Me to pour through them,
My Love would then be shaped
by the glory of their being
and delivered perfectly
as the gift of My Love
to bless and expand Creation.

The Longing for Love is a Spiritual Call

The longing for Love that is within you is not a weakness. It is not a lack of parental Love, or a void that was created that you are trying to fill. *Your longing for Love is placed in your heart by Me. It is your divine call. It is your homing device. It is the spiritual desire for your true home, for your right and real relationship with Me and with your true Love.*

It is a sadness to Me that this yearning I have placed within you is currently seen in this culture as a weakness. You are told that it makes you co-dependent, at worst, and less independent at best. So you turn away from your divine message, and you choose instead the messages of the ego as it seeks to create division. This distances you from what makes you whole.

Yet all the while people embrace these beliefs, the longing in the heart continues. It may be pushed away. But it is still there. This creates a war within, an internal battle that saps people of their strength, their vision, and most importantly, robs them of their spirituality.

In place of Love, people use drugs and alcohol — emotional abuse, emotional roller coasters, addictions to every manner of thing. Eating disorders. All of these things are designed by the ego to distract you from your desire for Love, or from your trying to reclaim that which you have sent away.

Alcohol can make you feel warm and supported. Drugs can give you back a contact with your spirit. But these things are yours naturally through Love. *Love opens your heart and restores your soul.* Love makes everything right in your world, not because it is a fantasy, but because *it brings you back in touch with Me. It places you in right relationship to your world with Love first.*

When you fall in Love you can see these connections. You are able to feel the life in everything. You find compassion for others because your heart is open. *Love is not a fantasy. Love is what is real. Everything else is the fantasy,* and not only a fantasy, it is a lie. It is a lie of the ego that leads you to believe you can live better without Love. The result is the world you see. The denial of Love in all its forms is what creates sickness and pain, despair and abuse. The more Love is denied, the "sicker" the society.

You must reclaim Love now. Do everything in your power to contradict the lies. Do everything you can to acclaim the truth of Love, not only in a broad sense as some nebulous belief, but in a personal sense in each individual's world.

In all the times where you have begun to believe that you were weak for wanting Love, I have said to you, "No! Hold on! Hold on to your belief in Love, no matter what. No matter what you see in front of you! No matter what you are told to believe." I promise you that it is only through the heart, through the restoration of Love, that humanity will be "saved." It is only by the restoration of Love that things can "right themselves," that all beings can be fed. They will be fed the food of the spirit as well as the food of the body.

Love is the only real food. Everything is fed by it. When Love is present and all things are growing, that growth is reflected on every level.

The path has split. The Love-less road is the path that you see if you look at the visible world. You know this. On a deep level you understand that all the hate, the crimes of human against human, parent against child, humanity against planet – every single one has at its core the loss of Love, the lack of Love, the emptiness and despair of a life and reality without heart.

The other fork is before you now, more and more visible and growing as hearts reclaim their ability to love. Yet to make the shift to this new Reality is going to take steadfast belief, unwavering, true, connected. It is going to take those whose hearts are connected and whose vision is clear, painting a picture again and again of life based in Love, and thus in Me.

You do know the words. You know the concepts. But it is in daily experience where your choices are made. Every moment. Not just the obvious choices of Love or fear, but the subtle choices to make Love the only priority in every moment. Personally.

It is in relationship that your choice is made.
Every moment is creation and the light is pouring in,
touching you. This light manifests your belief in that
moment, and the choices of your moments — what they
manifest when they are added together.

This is why you must have Love in front of you,
personified. The manifestation of the question of each
moment – what do you choose to create now? Please
make Love your answer! Please place Love above all the
things that you can allow to take you away from Love.

*Proclaim the reality of personal Love, of true
Love, of SoulMates. Proclaim the reality of Love that
will "fill the holes," supply the needs and bring you to
your center.* This is not weakness! It is not co-
dependence. It is Reality. Love is meant to make you
whole. What is wrong with that? Even when it begins as
an ego exchange, even if it looks "co-dependent"
(whatever that means!), it is worth it. Why? Because
one moment of real Love can change everything. Two
moments can heal everything. Three moments and
suddenly it is all revealed! The ego is seen for what it is.
The heart is chosen as the couple's reality and suddenly
they have shifted worlds. Suddenly they are living in the
New, the world of Love, waiting for humanity to claim
it. All who judged their relationship are still waiting,
empty and alone, whether or not they are in a
relationship.

There is no risk in Love. There is everything to
gain, because Love brings its own healing. Not just the

healing of old pain, but the release from the ego – the awakening. In an instant, everything can be changed by Love.

Love is worth everything. Divine Love will always be personal. This is how the universe works. Do you realize this? Everything you are; everything you need to learn comes to you in the "lessons" of your life. Surely Love would not be any other way. Love can only bless you.

If you understand Love, if you can open up and allow it to touch you, you will know that a moment in true Love gives yourself back to you. It reconnects you, gives you the experience of your heart, shows you your center, changes you, grows you, and even offers you the transformation of your being into an awakened human being. To turn this away out of fear is absolutely absurd.

People who are not in a relationship close themselves down out of fear of being hurt, or fear of not finding the "right one." People who are in relationship find thousands of ways to turn away, to keep distance between them, to be critical or irritated or whatever it takes. This is all ego, fighting to keep itself alive. Ego wants to keep you believing that fear is more powerful and that Love can hurt you. Once you understand the truth, the big picture, you will understand just how absurd this is. Love is your highest truth, the essence of your being, your connection with Me. Your communion with all life, the language of your soul and all Creation – to think that it is better to avoid it is beyond insanity!

There are so many things I want to show you. Every one of them requires an awakened heart. They require an understanding of the language of Love. So you see, even if all the "dangers" of Love were real, it would still be worth it, because it would give you access to Me. Directly. Clearly.

So even if you shared a brief time of Love with someone, the experience of Love in that time, if you allow it, could give you access to guidance that could teach and lead you the rest of your days. But listen to this! Like attracts like (you know this). So even a moment of real Love attracts more real Love! Now in your limited view this would mean that experiencing Love with one person would then attract the next person with whom you could have even deeper Love.

But the truth is this. The experience of Love attracts the true being, the real Love of that person in front of you so that they become more able to love, more full of light, more available to you. Then as they reflect this kind of Love to you, loving you this way, you are then able to open more deeply to Love. You gain access to your true self, and your relationship blossoms. In other words, when you choose true Love, true Love will be there.

The person before you will become ever more beautiful, more filled with light, more open, more connected to Me. As they love you like this, you will blossom also. Suddenly you will realize that a higher Love than you ever dreamed is before you. Form follows Love. The world you experience also follows Love. This is the New World. This is what you will find when you can "see" with your heart.

Thus, I ask this of you. *Take the leap to Love.*
Daily. Moment to moment. In doing this, I promise you
that you are changing the world. Those who love "the
whole world" will not change anything, nor will they be
changed. No, Love is personal, right in front of you. Only
thus will you change your experience of everything.

To make these choices for Love is something that
will take effort until your vibration is higher/faster than
that of ego (your heart chakra or above). It is a lot like
gravity. You must create enough velocity to break free and
then it is easy. Think of how much fuel it takes to fire
rockets that will take a capsule beyond Earth's atmosphere
into space. It takes a lot. A hot, hot fire, a lot of fuel.
Awesome power. This is what it will take from you also to
choose Love. But your heart knows this truth and it
wants to make the journey. This time in human history
means, essentially, that "gravity" is lessening. It is now
easier and easier to "blast off" than it ever was before,
because you are entering the Age of Homecoming.

It is the reminder of these words, this light and the
unwavering belief in Love shared over and over and over
that will give people the "push" they need to break
through the atmosphere of illusion – to get free of the
gravity of ego and to enter the larger universe (literally!)

It is to this end that I call you. *Believe in Love*
above everything. Once you can touch Me and grasp this
truth, once you can peek out beyond the atmosphere of
ego into the rarified atmosphere of life-changing beauty,

then together you can fuel the journey. Through LoveMaking, which is the most powerful "booster rocket" there is, as well as the most perfect tool of creation, you will fuel your journey. You will look into each other's eyes, and seeing the truth, yours and the truth of Love back and forth, back and forth, you will be free, together, in the realm of heart. It is meant. Two hearts together are the key. If you look together, you will see the path Home. *Take the leap. Open your heart, one to the other.*

What you must understand is that the person you are with will change as you change. He or she will blossom before your eyes and will match you, heart to heart, mind to mind, soul to soul. That person before you will come to embody your SoulMate energy. The truth of your union is the fact that having one person allows you the trust and the safety to blossom and to bring into form your highest truths. This person will mirror Love, delight you, challenge you, expand you and bless you. It will be a rainbow path rather than something little and gray. It will be a doorway to the universe, the path to the integration of your heart and soul. This path is as far beyond limits as you can get because it is right relationship. *It is the SoulMate consciousness. It is two halves of a whole, reflecting to each other what each is missing in order to be a fully aware child of God (a child of Mine!).*

The relationship of true Love between two people is the most freeing relationship ever created. Believe in it, in Love, in your soul, in your mate, and you will be reclaiming your divinity.

Now, one last important thing for those who

cannot yet choose this path of two. If you cannot yet believe in this, even if you do not feel you have found "the one," I still ask you to take the leap. Love fully even if you believe it will "end." In truth it is all one anyway (there is no way to explain this yet at your level). *Your journey to your SoulMate is one journey, no matter how many faces you believe it has. So dive in.* Love as if it were he or she. Refuse the belief that Love will hurt you. Know that every moment that you open your heart, you evolve. You reclaim your truth and every moment you love, you bring your true Love closer.

The more you can stay out of ego in your relationship, the clearer this will be. You may even be able to transform that very relationship into the one of your dreams, as long as it is your heart that is dreaming and NOT your ego. This is the critical choice you must make.

Once you realize that the ego will never allow you true Love and will never be satisfied with any person, you can begin the move to your heart. That move will stop the "search" and begin the transformation. A journey begins with a single step. True Love begins with a single decision – to choose to love by the heart.

What you will learn about Reality will shake you. It is nothing like you think. But what you learn about Love will wake you. Free you. It will bring Me to you in the most personal way – in the eyes of your beloved. On the lips of your beloved. In the heart of your beloved. Dear ones, that is where you will see Me!

Are you willing to allow your true Love in? Are you willing to allow your dreams to come true? Are you ready to live in a world rich in meaning, deep in profundity, glorious in its connection to every aspect of Reality? Yes? Then let us go together to the mirror of your SoulMate. There you will see Me in new ways.

It is a belief in Love
that surpasses every other thing in your life.
It is a desire for Love before which all else pales.
It is the assumption of Love – the knowing it is there.
It is awakening to your first breath
being a prayer for Love –
that this day will be the day
you truly experience it.
It is falling asleep in gratitude
for every gilded moment in which
Love shone upon you.
It is the taste of Love upon your lips –
not only in the kiss of your beloved,
but also in the passion of your words.
Every time you speak about the truth of Love,
the power of Love,
the perfection of Love,
those words crossing your lips are My kiss.
Every time you share your conviction,
every time you speak this truth,
you affirm My reality.
And in so doing,
you bring Me into your life.

The Definition of a SoulMate

In all of the dances of the soul throughout Time, there are many shades of personality, many forms and faces, and many characteristics in which a soul is cloaked for learning. In truth, each of these personalities is a "finger" of the light of the soul, dipping into Time to grow in ever-deepening individuality.

Some of these "fingers" will be cloaked as a woman and some as a man. For every personality expressing a soul, there is also the personality expressing the SoulMate. They dance together in ever-deepening awareness of Love in all its splendor, in all of its forms. The soul has no gender and the Love between SoulMates is eternal. Thus when true Love is brought fully into form, the awakening has no criteria for gender upon it. Love is Love, and Love is the foundation of Creation. Love is the essence of humanity.

In the awakening of Love in the world there is an expansion occurring that is far beyond gender. Because of the time of humanity, people are coming into incarnation with the express purpose of manifesting the SoulMate relationship in form. Why? Because the understanding of this relationship is the experiential form of the awakening.

Let me put this differently. The entire physical reality is for the embodiment of humanity's growth and awakening. It is spiritual school in physical form. Everything you learn will be manifested in your life.

Consequently, you can first see that *absolutely everything you have gone through has been for the express purpose of either your awakening or your service to the awakening of humanity.* Nothing else. Once you understand even this one fact, you can completely and quickly shift your thinking about all the things that "happened to you." Once you can fully accept and learn from this awareness, this relieves the future from any re-creation of the past or creation of the effects of the past. This is a fundamental and urgently important shift needing to occur everywhere. As you are discovering with everything, this too is another choice of the perspective of ego. Instead of saying "I'm wounded. This was done to me. I blame someone," you can now say "Thank you, God, the Creator, for the blessing of that learning."

If everything you experience is the manifested form of your learning, and humanity is on the cusp of moving into the heart, how would that be manifested in form? It is obvious. It would be manifested in form intimately, as your Love relationship. *Consequently, those who are what you could term "most ready" or "most advanced" are here to personalize Love and to live the SoulMate experience. In doing this, they are shifting to the heart and unlocking the energy of the New World.*

In committing to the SoulMate relationship and in choosing the manifestation of true Love, these people lift themselves so that they are functioning in the heart. They are seeing the world with the heart and thus, seeing the real home of humankind. Of course, as each person does this, it also lifts the vibration of the whole, giving the entirety of humankind a "boost." It creates an energy pathway for others to follow.

Now, if the goal of more and more souls now incarnated is to embody the truth of Love in form, then the ego energy is going to pull in the opposite direction. This is why there is so much cynicism and such an intense focus on independence at this time, as well as so much societal "preaching" about pampering the little "me, and getting more, more, more.

What we have right now is the ego's "backlash" fully in place, and the emergence of the souls seeking true Love not yet emerged. It makes it look a little grim sometimes. But I tell you, dear ones, the energy is here for the recognition of true Love as the spiritual path home.

You are made in My image and I brought you into individuality to reflect Love back to Me. I understood My longing and this need of an aware consciousness being able to see itself reflected back in Love. Therefore, I created this for you when I created you.

Even these words – "I created you" – are very limited. In truth, you came forth out of an awakening of Love within Me that by its nature brought you forth. The longing I had within for a consciousness and a heart that could surprise and enlighten Me brought you into both form and evolution. It was a cosmic LoveMaking in which everything that was Creation was touched and moved together. It brought forth someone who could see Me as I could see them, someone who could love Me as I love them. It was My heart embodied.

I will be telling you more of this explosion of Love, this experience of My own awakening that brought you into being.

So, in giving you life, I also gave you that greatest gift – the gift I longed for so much that I also longed for it for you. It was the gift of someone who was part of you, yet also an individual — someone who could reflect yourself to you and who also could surprise and delight you. Someone whose existence expands your being, and together you expand Creation. It is your SoulMate. *Your SoulMate is to you what you are to Me.* If you want to understand your SoulMate, read this again and let it speak in your heart, not in your mind. If you are in relationship, opening to your SoulMate before you, read this again. If you are longing for your SoulMate, wanting to bring him or her to you, read this again. Read it with your heart.

Your SoulMate is real. Your SoulMate is the key to your awakening and to the mystery and truth of Love. Your SoulMate is always with you but only when you can see with your heart, can you see him or her. This is one of the most important things I will say to you. As you are ready to be the embodiment of Love, you will be with him or her. But you could look with your ego for a million years and never see your SoulMate.

Now, because this relationship is so important at this juncture of humanity's journey, it is imperative that the SoulMate message become your focus quickly. Because this awareness is "built in" to your heart, as soon as most people hear this truth, they will recognize it. They will recognize it because they have always known. Always.

As you came into being, along with My desire that you have a gift in another as you are giving Me, the wholeness of your creation was exactly this. You were as I have said "two as one." The yin-yang symbol is the symbol of the SoulMate relationship. That symbol is what you looked like as an "embryo" – you and your SoulMate. You were wrapped together exactly like that, and you were like that in energy also. Because your purpose together was to be co-creators, there was a need for a "polarity" of sorts so that energy "sparking" between you would be strong enough to bring forth life.

Now that energy is absolute. One of you is "yin," the other "yang;" one is a plus and one is a minus. However, this is in the wholeness of your soul connection. The form in which you cloak your "fingers of light" (incarnations) as you manifest in Time does not matter. It is the energy of your soul that is what you have labeled male and female. Yes, the physical male and physical female bodies do generally reflect this, but not necessarily perfectly. The ego's version of "man and woman" is very different from the soul's yin and yang.

In this time on the planet, the most pressing issue, besides moving into the heart, is moving beyond judgment. This is a natural function of moving into the heart. It is opening the boundaries and restrictions of consciousness that have "held you in." Because of this, some people are manifesting their SoulMate relationship in same sex relationships. It does not matter. It is the heart and the soul that are important. If there is a lesson to be learned that can be accomplished through a same sex relationship, or if there is fear that can be circumvented by a same sex relationship, then this is what the soul will choose.

The objective is Love. However it can best be accomplished is fine. Dear ones, your bodies are only the dense form of your energies. There are many ways that some of these relationships balance some of the distortions of the ego that have been prevalent.

There is another important aspect of these same sex relationships which is becoming more and more obvious. They are widening the view of the consciousness of "society" so that even the ego is stretched to accommodate a larger view. So, for many reasons, many SoulMates are manifesting as same sex partners. Thus, a woman who has so much fear about men that she cannot access her heart (very prevalent in your society), will call her SoulMate to her in the form of a woman so that she can get past the fear.

Your hearts know that this is the time, that

Love is important, and that Love is personal. So your soul will "plot the best course" to get you there as fast as possible. Because your SoulMate becomes embodied as you become Love embodied, if you cannot "see" your SoulMate in one form, that form can change.

You'll notice that many people, particularly women who have expressed themselves heterosexually, will suddenly find themselves falling in Love with a woman. They are surprised. It is not as though they planned it that way. It is because they had too much fear to allow their hearts to be open to a man, and their SoulMate wanted to come through. Something in such a woman was open enough to call that Love to her, except for that one block of fear – so the soul circumvented the block.

Love is the priority. Nothing else, for once you are in your heart, you will draw everything else to you based on Love, based on the vibration of the heart. Based on the integrity of the heart. This will bring the Real World into view.

So, people must take in these truths quickly. Do not only hold on to the dream of your SoulMate but pursue it by learning to see and love in the heart. This Love is your personal way home – back into your relationship with Me.

As you reflect your deepest capacity for Love, living Love daily with your SoulMate, then by understanding Love in action and Love in form, you will begin to understand your relationship with Me. I tell you that looking into your SoulMate's eyes will show you the truths of eternity. There is only one thing you need to know about this truth. It will be "written" in the language of the heart. ***Dear ones, the language of the heart IS the language of eternity.*** It is the vibration of what is Real. Everything "below the heart" (everything of slower vibration) is illusion. It is temporary. It is here only for your learning until you are individualized enough to reflect Me, rather than be Me.

So speak the language of the heart and place before you the honoring of your dreams of Love. Those dreams are the voice of eternity, penetrating the illusion of the world of Time. "I am here," your SoulMate calls to you. Your answer should be: "Yes! I am waiting with an open heart." Do not believe the ego. Learn to see and to know with the heart, and your SoulMate will reflect that truth to you – that you are ready to take your place in eternity.

*A conscious world must have
participation from every part.
And a conscious human,
respecting that dialogue,
creates with Love and Wisdom
what supports this
glorious living universe.*

Only When Finding/Being the SoulMate is the Priority, Will Everything Fall Into Place

As the veils of time fall away, you will see the world revealed to you in its wholeness. You will see even the staunchest supporters of "individualism," of separatism, coming face to face with the need for unity, wholeness and inclusion. There are many ways for this to be learned. One is the opening of human hearts to My call — opening to the awareness of Love as your highest priority — opening to the understanding of the whole which is given richness and depth through its many parts, diversity as the foundation for union.

The other possibility for the understanding of the wholeness of this Earth/human system is through what you would term catastrophe. Humanity could come face to face with the results of current thinking and action. There could appear shortages of food, an ecosystem collapsing from the strain of trying to support a burgeoning population's interest on getting and not on giving.

Thus, I give to you the awareness of your magic— the picture of our intention as we moved forth together into physicality. *I call you to remember the perfection of Love that you are — the perfection of the Love I have for you and the choice of Love that is before you now.*

Always I hold forth your highest truth, for I know who you are. I know who you are intimately for you are part of My being, cells of My own heart, and this world that supports you is the manifestation of My Love in form.

In the beginning was the One. Then came the One that is Two. The cells of My heart were given polarity within the cell from which to generate creative energy. Each cell thus charged became the SoulMates — the one being that is actually two. They are two who can dance the dance of individualization; of awakening to co-creation, by reflecting their divinity to each other, and by generating the energy of creation between them.

Then, for the stage for the dance came the Earth — the embodiment of physical support and all the intricacy of life upon it. Dear ones, when I dreamed the Earth it was in such joy! It was the joy of knowing that you, My children, would be growing here. Nurtured here. Expanded here. What would be worthy of a consciousness such as yours? Only the most amazing, most beautiful and the most diverse environment possible. You are Mine, and not only did I want to delight you, I wanted to stimulate your growing consciousness. So I dreamed of rainbows, of beauty that begot beauty, of life in the most diversity that one system could hold. Certainly you have looked at the profusion of life on this Earth and wondered at its immensity. From bacteria to butterflies, everything was interconnected in a glory of communion, of interdependence and diversity unmatched anywhere.

Everything was created to stimulate, enlighten and

support you. Everything. Consequently, you affect everything. You, My children, were set down in a garden of such intricacy that you still do not comprehend all of it. And everything is connected to your learning, here to support you. Here to assist you in your growing abilities, and here to embody for you your energy and your attitudes and My support for you. There are many things to be said about this, and you can feel a number of them all extending from this moment. Focus here for today.

Here there is Love, in form — the one that is two, the positive and the negative that together express the nature of Love in form. These are the SoulMates. Around them is a world of unsurpassed beauty responding to their every need, reflecting to them My Love and giving form to their expanding consciousness. Every single part of this whole picture is in communication. This is the wholeness of the world.

So when you see your true Love's face, when you look into your SoulMate's eyes, you will remember all of this. You will remember that everything supports you. And everything is conscious. When you find the SoulMate Love, you will also find the key to communication with all the life of the world. You together will form the "HeartLink," that will allow you to speak, to see, hear, understand the real language of Love. Suddenly everything will not only "come alive" — everything will communicate with you.

This is how it is supposed to be! *The human union is the center of a sentient and supportive world.* Every face, every form on this Earth is teaching you and

71

supporting you. Not only symbolically. In real time, in real communication — through the language of the heart.

In reclaiming the SoulMate relationship first, everything else will open to you, because true Love will bring you into the realm of the heart where everything else will become known to you. I am telling you this to explain to you why *the SoulMate relationship must be the highest priority. It makes everything else work. It teaches you the language of the heart.* It opens you to seeing the reflection of your divinity and reflecting that to another. It exposes you to the real life understanding of GIVING which is the most powerful force for movement in the world. In the SoulMate relationship lies the real creative power of humanity.

Within the circle of Love that is the cell of My heart, the basis of Creation was given form. The cell became two, opposite charges — yet completely connected. All sexual union, all procreation anywhere and everywhere are the reflection of this original creation — your birth from within My heart into individuality. These two "charges" moving together, "sparking" between them, create the energy of Creation from which you, My children, form your own creations.

As above, so below. This original creation is reflected in billions of ways on billions of worlds but the original birth is you. My human children. And everything else created around you was created to support you. Because of your nature as co-creators with Me, you and I (All That Is, Was and Ever Shall Be) are the originators. New creation comes from us (or it will, when you reach maturity). All else is the expression of My joy! My joy as giving birth to you!

So rather than trying to convince people to save the world, rather than attempting to teach compassion, to somehow pull people beyond ego — rather than any of these approaches, first people must learn who they are. Who they are is Love, and that love is embodied for them, reflected for them, in their SoulMate. The SoulMate holds the key to understanding Love because he/she can show Love to you, in yourself where you have not seen it.

True Love opens the heart as nothing else can. True Love crosses all barriers, for every human heart has the longing for love. It is not like religion, where semantics and interpretations can completely occlude the truth. True Love speaks universally. In true Love the restlessness is finally stilled. The human longing is satisfied. Nothing else will do so. Nothing else, dear ones.

So, *until finding/being the SoulMate is recognized as the most important goal, the only real spiritual journey; until true Love is found, humanity will not have the attention to meet its goals, to transform reality.* I can promise you this because I created the longing. Until people understand the longing, they will keep following it unsuccessfully, not realizing it is an inner journey. They will search endlessly outside themselves. Until true Love is acknowledged as a worthy goal, the heart will remain hidden and the human will remain confused, because the heart is incessant in its longing. The dream will not go away. And as long as it is subverted by the ego, through its own messages, "Love is too dangerous!" "stay away!" or societal messages, "marriage is a social duty," or "marriage is doomed, bound to fail," people will be split apart. Their whole being cannot all go in the same direction, because the heart will never cease its yearning.

Yes! People can come directly to Me! They can have experiences of truth, of ecstasy, of awakening. But they still will not be love embodied until they are reunited with the other part of the whole. Yes, this message may be met with cynicism, even anger (the real source of which is having been forced to give up the dream), but in the end, the proof will be in the unfolding reality of Love, joy awakening and co-creation experienced by those who focus on true Love.

This is more than a spiritual path. This is the truth of Creation. If you do not believe Me, ask your heart. Honestly. And listen for the answer from your heart, not from your ego. You will know. You remember. *You remember this Love as surely as you know your own existence. You remember this Love, your SoulMate, just as a twin remembers the experience of another person with them in the womb. A memory of the most incredible closeness.* Of never being alone. Of two heartbeats in one womb, two beings as one reality. I promise you that this is true. Every part of your reality will uphold this.

Then, once this connection is made and is growing, the couples will see/hear/know the Love all around them. Animals, nature, every part of Creation will be alive in support. The opening of the heart to Love is the opening of the consciousness of the whole. Then the growth of awareness blossoming brings the experience of the New World of the heart. The Real World. Easily discovered, naturally. So I call you to Love first. Then everything else will open easily before you. More than "stewards" of the world around you, you are the center, the focus of it all. The moment your awareness switches and the heart becomes your medium of communication, everything else will come into view.

I return at times to the image of Adam and Eve in the Garden for if you understand this story on the level it was written, it is the story of Creation! Not "Eve made from Adam's rib," but the two in the beginning, surrounded by total support of nature. Everything was provided. Everything was speaking to them. The serpent, the "kundalini," the force of life within. The Tree of Life — the journey of humanity — the journey to individuality and co-creatorship. Outside of the Garden is the world of Time.

Never "dominion," rather communion and responsibility, you are responsible for this, your home, given to you in joy, affected by your consciousness, always supporting you in the journey by reflecting back your energy.

As soon as you remember, everything will return to harmony. And the path to remembering is Love — personal, embodied. The key to your heart. So I place before you the path home. The key to the awakening. A key that is still recognized universally. *Say "yes" to Love!*

Say "yes" to the presence of your SoulMate. Say "yes" to Love as your highest priority. Real Love. Deep Love, heart opening, world changing Love.

Let it rock your world or gently teach you, but whatever you do, open yourself to it, and your SoulMate will manifest. Then you must use the key that he/she holds to open your heart and thus to right the world. By lifting your hearts you will bring the Real World into view — the world that reflects your Love, the world as it was created. That world is here, just as your SoulMate is waiting for you to be able to see it. I will assist you every step, and it is not far away. The real world, the embodiment of Love, the reflection of your Love in form is right here. All it takes is the faith to open your heart.

Keep exploring Love.
Keep exploring the return to your heart.
As you come to nourish
the Love within you,
you will come to see that it is connected
to what is seemingly outside of you.
Thus you will discover that
All That Is is a "hologram,"
and that all is present everywhere.
The Love you develop in your own heart
becomes the Love that you nourish
in all Creation.
Thus I am nourished
and grown
and loved,
and Creation is ever expanded.

Our SoulMate Is How We Can Experience God, Without Losing Our Individuality

I hold you in My Love every moment of every day. This Love is deeper than anything you can touch with your mind. It is more profound than anything you can imagine in your biggest dreams. Love is movement. It is alive in the grandest form. It is beauty unfolding in everything from universe to atoms.

I Am this Love, and you live, grow and have your being within it. It is never ending. How then can you know this Love? You can know it because it is personal. Everything is conscious. Everything in its unfolding is aware, alive, awake in Me. In fact, everything besides you is always and forever fully aware in Me.

How can this be, you ask, that you are the crown of Creation, the manifestation of My Love? It is so because only you have the ability to turn away. Only you have free will. Only you can be, like Me, creators of all that is new and unique.

I Am personal. The fullness of My being is present in everything. Yet I need the reflection of your awareness to give Me the "distance" I need to see Myself in new and different ways. And I want the joy of surprise as I see you create — the delight of something new that I did not imagine.

If you are this to Me, the mirror in which I can see Myself as you dance, how then can you see? What gives you the reflection that you need to understand yourselves in Love? To touch Love, to experience Love? As I have said to you, every part of Creation is personalized, embodied Love – on absolutely every level. You know the answer to this question in your heart. You know there is another person that brings that awareness, that fulfills you. This is what you call your SoulMate. Yet, in this unfolding glory of Love, what does that mean to you, here, now, in this time of change in the world?

Drop now from your mind to your heart and let Me speak to you of Love. It is only in the heart that you can hear this. You are one who is two in order to know The One. Truly if you come to Me directly, you will be absorbed in this Love. It will be ecstasy. It will be home – but home in a way that removes from you your unique ability, your perspective and your Will. Were you to come to Me directly with your heart completely open, you would cease to be. You could not stay individualized because you would know Me too deeply. You would recognize that which is you is also that which is Me – to such a degree that you would melt in bliss back into the Oneness of My All.

This is not why I created you. You were born of My desire to know Myself in new ways. You were born of the longing in My being for company! It is true. In all of Creation, all things are within Me. There was nothing I could look upon that had any distance. Nothing could show Myself to Me. It was like trying to know yourself by observing a cell in your kidney or a corpuscle in your blood. So you emerged from My desire to deepen My experience and to bring forth progeny, and thus, surprise! As all parents know, you were born from the spark of My longing, igniting the process of creation in My heart.

This process of creation is a process of two forces creating a spark between them that brings forth new life. Those two forces of life, forces of Love – that is you and your SoulMate or Twin Flame.

Now you are here, poised on the planet of rebirth, awaiting your inclusion in The All as individuals. How can you know who you really are, now that it is time? How can you understand your true being and your relationship with Me, when you cannot know Me directly in the very deepest sense? How can you maintain your precious individuality – the individuality that this whole Earth/Time experience has been for? The answer is by looking into the heart of your Twin Flame. That is how I created you, with a guaranteed avenue for understanding Me, for experiencing who you are as My child – through the reflection of your true heart in the experience of your true Love.

"Oh, sure," you are saying. "Right. True Love. How many people still believe in that?" What I say to you is that everything is changing. Your vision is clearing all the "smokescreens" that have been in place to protect you as you grew, to support you in your individualization. All of these are fading. In the light of the New, your true Love will be there.

I don't want you to wait. Don't think this is a fairy

tale. Instead, ask for testimony from your own heart. Have you not always known this? You have. There are two really important things to remember. The heart sees completely differently from the mind or the ego. And, the fastest way to leap into the New is through the experience of reclaiming this shared heart, and thus reclaiming your most intimate relationship with Me. Remember that this being is the way that you can truly know Me!

Some of you have been able to see with your heart enough to know your destiny and to recognize your Twin Flame as they are incarnated before you, but very few. Because this experience is the most direct route to your return home, your return to your place as co-creators – individualized, yet fully in my heart – I ask you to make this a priority.

What of people who are happy single? What of those who look and look and cannot find this being? What if you are with someone but can't imagine that person is the one? What if, what if, what if…? *Listen.* *Your SoulMate is always with you.* Always! You cannot be apart. You are two halves which together create far more than a whole being! How can I tell you this? When you are together, universes fly forth. Stars are born. Love is given shape by your shared desire. Oh, dear ones, you have no idea yet, because you have been "locked away" in one dimension (yes, really this is only one), and you cannot see yourselves yet.

You have always heard, "when the student is ready, the teacher appears." On the same note, *when*

your heart is ready, your SoulMate appears. Not
because they have not been there! But because you have
been unable to recognize them. The moment you can
"read" with your heart you will recognize them. I will
say to you that once you are able to see them and to
reach conscious agreement on this thick and difficult
"physical" level, in that moment your universe will
change. Now in that moment, when you commit to
living as SoulMates in the heart, from the heart,
choosing to go beyond ego – in that moment you come
into real contact with Me. Not simply on an
informational level. No, you begin to live in Me, and
everything in your life will shift. Things will "fly to you"
that show you My being, My truth and give you the
experience of My Love through your ability to look into
the eyes and heart of another. You will begin to
experience true Love.

True Love is beyond Time. True Love exists in
the reality of My heart. It is absolutely never restricting.
Oh no, rather it is a doorway into the biggest, the most
vast, the endless experience of My Love as co-creators.
Yes, you can create separately (without knowledge of the
other – for they are there whether or not you know it),
but I tell you this. Once you are united consciously with
your SoulMate, then you are ready for real co-creation –
the moment your hearts are engaged.

Forms come and go. The closer you are to your
SoulMate, the more intimately you know Me, the less
"physical" your world will be. It will become the
dancing "molecules" of light it really is, and your co-
creative Love will easily create with it.

If you are with someone, look with your heart and you will see your SoulMate there! How can this be, you may ask, and then you list all the "things that are wrong." I tell you how. Your heart is ready if you are aware of this. You would not have drawn in anyone else. You have simply been looking with the wrong eyes. If you can see them, they will begin to see you. As the millennium changes, you will find you are with the person you are meant to be with in the New World.

Being with your SoulMate is a decision, a decision to use the only "organ of sight" with which you can see your SoulMate, your heart. As many times as you slip back into your ego, that many times you will fail to see what Love can be. You will lose your blessed connection with your true experience of Me and of yourselves as co-creators. As many times as you remember, that many times will you find your heart, your mind, your being filled with joy, with the surety of My deep and personal Love and with the experience of yourselves, awake and alive in all of Creation, co-creating All That Is!

Oh, yes, there are mysteries here! Mysteries of how suddenly you can see your Love, your mate when even a moment ago you could not. Mysteries of how, suddenly, the moment you move into your heart, you are totally fulfilled, gloriously blessed, deeply and profoundly in Love. Mysteries that speak to the deepest longing of your soul and mysteries that answer the questions of eternity. That "mystery" is the truth of the heart.

In one moment you could be facing your Love, feeling filled with an endless list of grievances and shortcomings. You could be making Love with the other part of your soul and feel alone, if you are in the ego. And this is what happens day after day in life after life. Your ego will never let you see your true Love. Never. Please understand this. Because when you see your true Love, the ego's job is totally done. It will automatically begin to fade until you live so deeply in your heart that the ego is a thing of the past.

Only when you move to your heart can you see true Love. Only when you see through your heart can you recognize your truth – that this Love will always reflect to you your highest truth, which is your existence as co-creators in Love. *Your SoulMate is the mirror I have given you so you can know yourself and so you can know Me.*

Your SoulMate is with you, has always been with you, simply cannot be without you. Your SoulMate has been drawing you, guiding you, whispering to you all your life. If you are not seeing your mate, switch to your heart and wait. He or she will quickly appear. But remember, switch back to your ego and he or she will disappear again!

If you think you are alone, then right now, this moment, as humanity rides the cusp of its awakening, he/she is walking toward you. If you are looking with the right vehicle, first you will see his or her heart. Then you will see things form. If you are awakening and you are with someone, that person is it. You have drawn them. In this time of the world, believe Me, the wholeness of each being, the two halves have been drawn together.

Not seeing it? Hmm. Looking with the wrong eyes? Only if you are someone who has been asleep, totally shut down to Love, could you have drawn to you someone whose vehicle cannot accommodate the higher vibration of your SoulMate's presence. This person must learn to see with his/her heart and look very carefully. Then, if it is clear that there is no accommodating the new energy of real Love there, it may be necessary to draw in someone else.

As yet you cannot understand this, but as time goes on I will be able to explain how absolutely perfectly each moment is built. I will be able to explain to you how your SoulMate could incarnate right before your eyes, transforming someone you thought you knew (though wrongly) into the true Love for whom you have always longed. (The hint is that they were always there, of course.)

There will be those who ask whether having one mate will be limiting. I tell you this. If you find your true Love and you learn to share that Love in the realms of the heart, all of Creation will be your playground and the Love between you will be the greatest possible Love. There will be only ever-expanding discovery and only ever-deepening experiences of Love. The concept of limitation is a trick of the ego.

Reach out then. Say "yes"! With heart and soul, say "yes"! Then I can teach you the secrets of all life and reveal the magnificence of Love to you. Come reach across the starry sky that holds all the worlds and reach within the heart of God and welcome your Love to you.

Nothing has prepared you for this beauty. Nothing until this could reveal your glory. All you have to do is leave the ego, blessing it as you go for the individuality it gave you. Joining hearts, you can dance beyond Time into the world of Love manifesting through you. Then, reach out your hands together and bring others with you.

You are meant
to live each day totally
"head-over-heels in Love."
Every moment
should be a glory
because your Love is alive
in the world.

Give Yourself Completely to Love

Every moment is stepping "off the cliff," into the unknown. It is only your efforts to create continuity that make it seem otherwise. But in those efforts to name and thus "tame" the world — to know life, to create safety — you limit your possibilities. As long as you believe that you know, you will not really know. As long as you think there are boundaries to your world, you limit your experience.

So I ask you to jump off the cliff into My arms. My arms are the arms of Love. My reality is the reality of Creation. Without limit. Without end. Magic moment within magic moment. Beauty unfolding into beauty. I have wonders in store for you. I have life for you to live, filled with a richness of spirit, a depth of soul, a joy and awareness beyond your dreams. But in order to have all that I want to give to you, *you must trust the reality of Love.*

More than trust Love as reality, you must give your life to it. Make it your crusade. Be willing to give your life for it – in any way, for the life you will give is a life of limitation and pain. The life that you gain will be ecstasy and joy. Timeless. The reality of Love has no beginning and no end. It is not finite. It is your true home.

How many of you really trust in Love? Very, very few. To trust in Love is to trust in Me, for Love is what I Am. It is All That Is. Only in Love can you ever reclaim your truth, your heritage and your relationship with Me.

In this moment I ask you to give yourself completely to Love. I do not ask you to "believe" in Love but to know Love as your reality. Not to accept it as a future possibility, but to accept it as your truth, in this moment. Then in this moment. Then in this moment.

Rest in My Love. Let it hold you, sustain you. Let it support you. Touch the truth of its timelessness. Rest here with Me for a moment. But then, once rested, I ask you to take on the reality of Love in action — in your life, by living the embodiment of Love with another.

This, dear ones, is living your spirituality. This is "walking your talk," as you say – living in Love, being in Love every moment of every day. Believing that Love can transcend it all. Believing that if you choose Love, real Love, true Love, it cannot ever hurt you.

I ask you to choose, right now, to accept the embodiment of Love in your life. I ask you to make the choice to have true Love. *Courageously open your heart to whomever is there for you now, knowing that in doing so, you call your SoulMate to you. This means that as you love, purely, exuberantly, fully, spiritually in this moment, then Love will be more fully embodied before you in the next moment.*

If you live your life in fear, if you choose safety, you close off your truth. You shut out true Love. If you choose safety, believing this is not your SoulMate in front of you, or believing this person has the power to hurt you, then you are choosing ego, choosing fear,

choosing limitation, and your SoulMate cannot come
to you.

You already know that there are only two choices
– Love and fear. You know that Love is the truth and fear
is the lie. But what you have not really seen is how you
choose fear and pretend it is Love, again and again, daily,
moment by moment. You keep your heart locked away.

Until you open your heart, you will not know
Me. You will not have the key to the New World. You
will not allow your spiritual transformation. You can
only experience this transformation through the heart,
and you can only unlock your heart through Love.

Even you who believe you love, who believe you
are choosing Love, saying "yes." Are you? Really? If you
were, you would live every moment in the deepest most
profound joy. You would be in communion with
everything. Maybe not verbally, but you would feel in
your heart the resonance and the greeting of absolutely
every living thing.

*Choose to throw open your heart and to see
Love in front of you, no matter what your ego tells
you.* Here is the most profound truth. The ego tells you
lies. It holds up a "screen" in front of you upon which it
has painted a picture, and then convinces you that
picture is reality. Listen closely. Behind that false picture,
true reality exists. Right there in front of you. If you
refuse to believe the ego, it has to take down the screen.

You could believe the lies of the ego. You could

believe there is no one, or believe your current partner is flawed beyond hope, and right behind that image, your SoulMate exists. Right there. True reality. Waiting for you to look beyond the screen. How do you do this? By switching to your heart as the "organ" you "see" with. And how do you do this? By throwing open your heart and trusting Love.

If you do this, the embodiment of your true Love will appear. If you say "impossible" to this, and begin listing reasons, then you must know that the ego has you with its lies. Know, too, that I am here always, asking you in every moment, "will you choose Love"? When you say "yes" and switch to your heart by unlocking it, throwing it open, you will begin your path of the heart, your path to transcendence. No matter what is "playing" on the screen, if you continue to make the choices of Love, real Love, true Love, every moment you so choose, you connect with reality and bring it more into view.

Because Love is the truth, Love is reality. It must be your highest priority. Because the heart is the vibrational chakra, the perceiver of reality, your desire must be to live in the heart – to perfect your ability to speak Love, to see Love, to be Love. I Am Love. Thus when you choose Love, you choose Me. If you choose Love, everything else will be "added unto you."

Money is energy. If your energy is on the level of Love, the highest form of abundance will be yours. Money is one representation of this. It will flow to you. But so will perfect attunement in every situation. Doors will open. Things will appear, and as you move into

Love, you will be living beyond the false "screen" of the ego's reality. This is how you can live in the New World right beside those who are still in the old. You will both be looking at the same thing but you will both be seeing something completely different. You will see Love and beauty. They will see fear and lies.

Love is the doorway to the New World. Everything is embodied. All energies are conscious and all energies have form. The form of Love is your partner. You get to "find the secret code" and open the door. The secret code is your heart.

If it seems I am repeating things, it is always because I need to. I want to show you this truth, again and again, until you understand it. You will not know what is really in front of you. You can be staring right at your SoulMate and not see him or her at all. Your ego may be holding up a screen that says, "no one is here. I'm all alone." Right behind the screen, your SoulMate is waiting! As long as you look with the "eyes" of the ego, you will see the blank screen. Look with the heart, and your SoulMate appears. So if you are alone, begin communicating to your true Love. Open your heart. Choose Love. Every moment. Refuse fear. The more open your heart, the more clearly you will see until you are fully aware.

Remember that your SoulMate is a reflector for you. When you look, you will see "the state of your Love." If you are afraid, you will be with someone who is "shut down" or fearful. As you open your heart, they will open theirs.

If you are aware enough to be reading this, if this has come to you, your SoulMate is in front of you. If you refuse to believe it, you may have to "shake yourself awake," by causing things to happen around you or even "changing the face" of the being in front of you, but I tell you – he or she is there.

The main thing I am showing you is the consuming commitment that must be made to seeing Love, to living Love, to sharing Love. To moving Love. As you become more conscious, you will realize that you, My children, actually generate Love. When your hearts are open, there becomes more Love available in the world. This in itself will change things. However, once you are conscious of the energy of Love, its creation and movement, you can direct it with your Will. Thus, you become co-creators in Love. Co-creators with Me. Then, with Love, you can easily manifest together the life of your heart (not the life of your ego, for the vibration of the heart does not accommodate ego). And, by showing others the choice before them, you can open the door to the New World.

In Love you will always see Me. This I promise you. I am revealed to you intimately in the heart of your beloved. When you can experience the heart, you will experience Me. *Dedicate a relationship to me first and foremost, and you will automatically have the experience of Love.*

By asking you to choose Love, I am not asking you to put something "before" Me – for I am fully present at the level of the heart. When you open your heart, you have access to Me. To My tender Love. To My passionate joy. To my moment-to-moment guidance. Open your heart, and it will reveal Me to you. Thus, in your choice to love, moment-by-moment without fear, you create the ability to know Me personally.

I Am. I Am everything. I Am also fully present in everything. So every experience of Love leads you to Me. Every experience of ego places that same "screen" there. It doesn't change the fact of My presence but can make you believe you do not see Me.

You know — all who travel this path home — that daily you have choices. You receive "messages." Things are sent to you. When you reach the level of true Love, of the full and open heart, you will hear the entire dialogue. All of Creation "speaks Love." Everything will then "speak" to you. You already understand that there are those who can "hear," who can speak pieces of the dialogue. There are those who can hear animals. There are those who can see the spirit world. When you reach the level of the heart, all of Creation becomes understandable to you. It is in your daily life that you make the choices for Love that will bring you into the universal dialogue.

At the level of this truth, you can feel Me. You know that Creation is within Me. And floating, dancing, living, evolving in Me is every being, every atom, every world. All are alive, formed from Love and available to you through the understanding of your heart.

Dedicate your lives to Me. Choose true Love. Choose Love. Choose Love.

I say to you now
that it is imperative
that you open your heart,
your mind,
and your spirit
to the proof of Love in your life.
I ask you to understand
that Love must be standing in front of you,
as soon as you remember who you are.
As you turn your beloved faces
back to the light of
My presence.

Rush Headlong Into Love!

Trust Love. With all of your heart. With all of your soul. For in trusting Love, you are trusting your own highest nature. In trusting Love, you are saying "yes" to receiving all of the gifts of your humanity, all of the gifts of your divinity. Everything I have made is Love. In trusting Love and only in trusting Love, do you say "yes" to life!

Do you have any idea how many people cry in the night for Love, pray to Me for Love and then do everything in their power to deny it? How many people turn away when Love is standing before them? And why do they turn away? Why would someone shun the blessings their whole being longs for? Out of fear.

Dear ones, let Me tell you this. If ever there was a moment in which you make the choice – heaven or hell, good or evil, a God or the Devil – it is that moment. It is the moment when you look at the possibility of Love, and turn away. In that turning, you are spurning all of My gifts to you. You are turning away from your own destiny. I promise you this — EVERYTHING is based on the acceptance of Love. When you choose fear over Love, you turn away from everything that comes from Me.

Do you see how insidious fear can be? The subtle message of fear comes creeping into your mind with messages of self-preservation. It lives in your dreams, side-by-side with your longing for truth, for joy, for your SoulMate, and your desire to serve all that is good. And dear ones, I tell you this. *There are no degrees of fear. You choose fear or you choose Love.* It is time you understood this.

It is time for your hearts to return to their wholeness, time for the world to return to Love. You have gotten to experiment with separation. Now I call you back. Now at this time, the Homecoming, it is only the choices for Love that will get you there.

I come to you now, taking your hand, calling your name, beckoning your heart. I am whispering to you that all of your dreams, all of your goals, all of your visions hinge on this — the choice for Love. In these days of awakening, I ask you to look carefully at your moments and what you choose. So many of you live in fear that even your true Love cannot come to you.

Why would you want to protect yourself from Love? The belief that there is anything to fear from Love is the lie. First you must recognize that as long as you fear Love, you have not experienced Love, for Love and fear cannot exist in the same place. Please think about this.

Very few people have ever experienced Love! I shall repeat this. *Because Love and fear cannot exist in the same place, very few people have ever really experienced Love.* You have experienced only fear. You do not know Love. Rather, you know messages of fear that contain a reference to Love. These you mistake for the experience of Love. This lie is handed to you in your crib, in your mother's milk. It is received by your psyche long before you can speak. "Be careful," it says. "Love will hurt you." "We love you," goes the message, "so we want to protect you." So rather than going boldly into life with an open heart, every child is taught to guard his/her heart. To keep it closed. Thus, dear ones, you are taught not to live.

Now I have come to open your precious hearts. I have come to tell you that it is time to remember Love. It is in Love that you were created. Everything you are meant to have and experience is all based on Love. And it is all experienced through an open heart. So I now say to you that you cannot choose both fear and Love. I say to you, give Me one moment with your heart completely unguarded, and I will show you Love!

Knowing that only Love can draw more Love, you must look at every moment and see what it is you choose. As you choose Love, Love will appear before you. Love will come rushing to you. Like attracts like. The vibration of Love is the vibration of a world you have yet to see – your home. Love will be manifested before you in form. As you open to Love, you will see your SoulMate. Your true Love. But even when you have drawn this being to you, if you fail to choose Love, this being can still disappear! Because one moment you are seeing with your heart, and the next you have closed your heart in fear and you are seeing with your mind, with your ego. You are telling yourself the lie that Love can hurt you, and you are pushing your Love away.

Until you have chosen to love with an unguarded heart, you have no idea what Love is! Until you know what Love is, you cannot draw Love to you. So you are dancing through a hall of mirrors that is showing only your fear to you, and you are convincing yourselves it is Love. Then, based on this illusion, you decide that Love is not for you.

In these messages I have come to shake you. To awaken you. To say to you that Love is the most amazing, profound, incredible and glorious experience you will ever have. It is your destiny. And it is meant to be personal. Embodied. Right before you. Your heart continues to tell you this, in spite of all the ways you try to silence it.

In telling you that you have not experienced Love, I am asking you to take another chance. To recognize all the ways that fear controls you. All the ways you choose the lie, day after day, moment after moment. Recognize that all the things you have called Love have been fear in disguise. Raise the bar. Choose nothing less than true Love.

I have already told you that as you choose Love, your SoulMate will embody before you. In truth, they will become visible. They are already there. *What I am telling you this moment, is to RUSH HEADLONG INTO LOVE! Throw open your heart. Expect Love to support you, heal you, glorify you!* Revel in Love. Choose the heart. Look at what is before you and choose Love. When you do, Love will be revealed to you.

Suddenly your open heart brings the full power, light, focus of your soul. As your soul comes close, your SoulMate comes into view. Your open heart opens the heart of your partner, and what begins to be reflected back to you is your SoulMate at the level of heart, truth, reality, true Love.

What does this mean? *It means that whomever is in front of you IS your Soul Mate, reflecting your current beliefs about Love. Your partner is a manifestation of your Soul Mate as he/she appears at your current level of consciousness.* You are always with your Soul Mate, as your Soul Mate reflects your consciousness back to you in form. This may be very hard to swallow, but it is true. The Earth school is the experience of your awakening in form.

As you open and your heart touches your partner's heart, their opening heart will allow your SoulMate to more fully manifest before you. For now, you must trust Me on this. What I am saying to you is that you must examine your beliefs and decisions about Love from a new perspective. You must examine them from the perspective of a truly open heart. An absolutely fearless belief in Love. I come to you to say to you, CHOOSE LOVE! And to assist you in seeing when you do not. In those moments, you are making the choices that determine the course of the world.

Out of the creative matrix of the two, from the discovery of real Love alive in the SoulMate relationship, the reality of the world will easily change. The Love that is awakened is not only embodied in the relationship. It changes the vibrational reality of the world. Opening to Love is the first step to changing anything. This should be obvious to anyone who is looking at all.

The real human path
is about Love.
It is about energy
on the heart level and above,
the level of truth.
I absolutely promise you
that this is your path home.
It is the path to your awakening,
to the elevation of humanity.
This is why the longing for Love
is so powerful within you.

The Path of the Heart

Even now, when the sum of humankind is barely on the edge of awakening – even now, there are gems of intense beauty that shoot through, out of the gray of mass consciousness, straight into the light. These gems shoot into the hands of the angels whose job it is to amplify every human thought, prayer, desire or feeling that is based in Love.

As those gems of Love multiply, as you gain your "footing" in the New World, the new level of the heart, it will be like shooting stars. You will give blessings to Me as you learn to give to others and to live from the heart. Because every human consciousness is unique and every human heart is divine, when the two meet, everything in Creation is changed.

How then can you know what to give to others? How can you possibly know what you are even "seeing," if each consciousness is different from yours? Ah, yes, by communicating with the heart.

You can never understand how another person sees the world. That is meant to be a special unique thing, a part of Creation that is so sacred that it belongs to each human being making his or her contribution to the whole.

So, there is no way two people can understand

each other if they use the mind. It's not possible. Nor is it ever possible to link on the emotional level, because that level, while it gives interesting texture to the current world, that level is based in the ego. Thus it is not a reliable indicator of anyone's truth. *The only way two people can ever really meet is in the heart.*

Many of you are beginning to understand this. Two people can live for years in "different worlds." And in those worlds "men are from Mars and women are from Venus," and the two will never meet. On that level those books are helpful because they at least provide some acceptance of the "differences." But dear ones, those differences are not cultural, though they may be influenced by culture. They are not gender-based, though they may be influenced by hormones. Rather they are the result of a simple fact. *Below the vibrational level of the heart, everything is in the realm of ego, and ego's job is to separate you.* Remember this.

Ego will always separate you because that is what it was designed to do by Me. It is not a negative thing. It was a necessity. But no matter how much acceptance a couple may find in having a "road map" of ego, that is not what the heart is meant to have. So no matter how much acceptance or how many agreements a couple makes, they still will not be satisfied. They will not be happy, because they are still alone. And they are not meant to be alone! Until they learn to love with the heart, to communicate with the heart – until then they will always be unhappy. They will feel alone. A part of them will still be "looking" for that unnamed thing that will finally make them happy. They will be looking for some nebulous inner peace and fulfillment.

The reason there are so many divorces now is not that people don't take Love seriously. (Surprised, aren't you?) It is not that they don't have the gumption to stick with it. Do you know why many marriages now end in divorce? It is because the signals of your true nature, the glimmers of reality are stronger than before, because the veils are thinning. *People are more aware that there has to be something more. Their hearts are speaking to them!* But they do not have the information they need. So they wrongly assume that they can find what their hearts are showing them in a different person. So they try and try again and again. They go to counseling. They read the books. But they cannot get across the "divide." They cannot make the connection their hearts are pointing to. So they divorce yet again, believing they have not found their true Love, when in truth they have not learned how to BE true Love. They have not learned to communicate with the heart.

You are not meant to be alone. You are a part of two that is one. But you absolutely cannot experience this on any level below the heart because on those levels, it does not exist. The vibrational levels below that of the heart – what you would call the charkas of survival and ego – only access the limited world of your "childhood," the "safe place" of your developing. (Looking at the results of ego, you would not wish this on the rest of Creation, would you?) You are held tenderly here while you grow. But now, you see, the signal is arriving. The notice is given. "Awake!" it says. "Awake and be Love, live Love, have the dream."

Without understanding what it means in any conscious way, people feel it pressing them and pushing them to reach for something they cannot name. Because this is the time for humanity, the cusp of your awakening, *people cannot settle for life without Love.* But all they know is life without Love. They have no idea how to get that Love. Because they have only the ego-based reality to go by, they look externally to find what they need, trading partners frantically, and trying to assuage that longing in their heart.

So I bring these Messages to give people access to their heart. Then they will have the Love they have only had in their dreams, because they will finally be joined. They will finally be there with each other. They will know their destiny. In the moment they access their shared heart, they will return to the "Garden." They will be home with Me! As they share and amplify their Love, the angels will assist. Soon their hearts will lead the way, not their ego, and suddenly they will begin to see a New World coming into view.

Oh, dear ones, people do need to understand this. *Nothing will work for any couple in the long run except Me and the connection of the heart.* The entire search of your whole life is for this connection. All the things that people "blame" their partners for, everything people think they deserved – every bit of it has been the search for this Love.

Parents are not supposed to love their children in the way children now believe they should. That is for their SoulMate to do. Even this current wave of therapy and all the blaming of the parents, this too is the misinterpreted call of the SoulMate message. *People know they should have this kind of Love – a Love in which they are finally truly seen, totally loved, held in perfection in another's eyes.* Remember why I created you? So you can mirror Me, show Me Myself in new ways — another equal consciousness, looking back, mirroring perfectly. That is what your SoulMate is for you!

Theories abound that say that this is the parents' job. "Complete Positive Regard." These theories say that if a baby looks at his or her parents and does not see this positive regard, then they shrivel in some way. They don't have confidence. I say to you now, it is not the parents' job to do. That is the purpose of your SoulMate. If a child knew that such a mate was there for him or her, it would give them that confidence. It would also allow that SoulMate to come to them quickly. There would be no mistakes, no lost relationships of "broken hearts." Children would be "putting that signal out there" all their life so that, like a homing beacon, it would draw the SoulMate. They would not draw some other skewed relationship based on the belief that "they really don't need anyone," while their hearts cry out every day for true Love.

So it is not the parents' job to love a child as the SoulMate does. Because they can't. *Two people who are SoulMates do literally share a soul.* They are the yin and yang, the plus and minus rolled into one. No one else can mirror this to another.

So, the entire picture of reality changes when the

longing in the heart that every person carries is acknowledged clearly. People must learn to see with their heart so that they will be able to see their mate. Dear ones, *your SoulMate is right in front of you but they exist in the REAL world, the world of the vibration of the heart or above.*

So what can couples do to reach their hearts?

Meditation. They must make a place in their life for listening. Without this we cannot proceed. I have to have their opening. I cannot be fully present in their relationship unless they ask Me to be. Then, if they want guidance, they must listen for it.

Prayer. One of the most important connections two people can make is shared prayer. The act of praying together is a powerful statement – not only to Me but to themselves and to all the loving beings that surround them. Remember that I said that all the rest of Creation supports you! However, you must allow this support. As a result of your gift of free will, you must ask on some level of your being before you can receive. If you don't ask, you are basically "hands off" to all who could help you.

Upgrade to the heart. The experiences of the heart should be honored and can be recorded in a "journal of the journey of awakening" for the couple. For those who are ready, they should participate in a sacred wedding or commitment ceremony that will delineate a shift that will speak to every level of their being and to all those who assist them.

Language. They must have a complete shift in the language they use, being very careful, especially, about the words they use to speak about their relationship.

Open to joy. Approach everything as a potential source of, or opening to joy. Any crisis a couple is experiencing is the most amazing blessing because it means that their hearts have gotten through to them. They are about to fall in Love again in a way they have never yet experienced. Falling in Love is a glimpse through the veil into true reality.

Learn to distinguish between the ego and the heart. The more deeply their hearts are connected, the more support they will have for making their relationship flourish in Love.

They must joyfully accept all of this as easily done and already being accomplished, even while they take the steps to implement it. Refrain, carefully, from making it difficult. The heart's view of Time is that of eternity. All things, right here NOW. The ego's version of time is linear.

In My hands, you have everything. In your Love you can know Me intimately. You come to understand my gifts by living them together. Practice "walking on air." Know you are held up, sustained, every moment, even though you may not "see" what sustains you.

I am with you. In your heart you will see Me. In your hearts you will know Me – together, as you are meant to see, magnifying My Love. The circle of Love – of your being together as the two being one — is yours to claim.

Let Me show you how,
surrounded by the blossoming expression
of My being that is Creation,
I longed to be seen,
to be known.
To have relationship.
To understand Myself
through the vehicle of being in relationship.
Because all Creation was within Me,
there was no one I could "see eye to eye."
No one with whom I could interact
for a sense of Myself.

This longing swept through all Creation.
Out of this longing came the growth of My heart
into individuated cells,
into beings who were My progeny.
As this formation occurred in My heart's cells,
I knew that each of My beloved children
must have what I so longed for.

Each of you must have holy relationship.
Divine relationship.
Relationship that reflected your truth
as you could see yourself.
Instantly from this awareness came
the division of each cell of My heart into two —
so each part could be fully in relationship
with the other.
I could be in relationship with you!
Thus in all the heavens,
the systems within systems,
there was intelligence equal to Mine.
Intelligence to grow Me.
In each intelligence,
each cell of My heart,
there was that same blessing –
equal intelligence,
actively in relationship – moving,
sparkling and growing each other.
Two beings in one cell.
Twin sparks of life substance.

The Truth of Love In the New Millennium

The texture of Love is far richer, the passions of Love far greater, the truth of Love far deeper than you have ever known.

I want you to vow to find it, to know Love as you have never known it, to feel Love as you have never felt it, to be blessed by Love as you have never been blessed. This is to be your quest. This is the Holy Grail of the New World. It is My call to all hearts in the new millennium. The key to your success is believing. Not faith. Not "hoping in things unseen." No.

The key is absolute conviction. It is a belief in Love that surpasses every other thing in your life. It is a desire for Love before which all else pales. It is the assumption of Love – the knowing it is there. It is awakening to your first breath being a prayer for Love – that this day will be the day you truly experience Love. It is falling asleep in gratitude for every gilded moment in which Love shone upon you. It is the taste of Love upon your lips – not only in the kiss of your beloved, but also in the passion of your words.

Every time you speak about the truth of Love, the power of Love, the perfection of Love – those words crossing your lips are my kiss. Every time you share your conviction, every time you speak this truth, you affirm

My reality. In so doing, you bring Me into your life.

Love in one moment can do more than thousands of prayers. Love can heal you. It can lift you. It can take the blinders of ego from your eyes. It can unfetter your heart and bring it wings. As Love bestows its blessing upon you, brought forth by your belief, your world will be changed, your life will be changed and your relationships will be changed. Like rain in a desert, Love called forth by your conviction will nourish everything around it. As the desert after a summer rain, all hearts, all lives will burst into bloom around you, if your Love is true. And you need not love any of them directly, for just as surely as rain brings flowers, Love brings the blossoming hearts. It is a law – physical and spiritual, emotional and mental. Where the blessing of Love falls, everything it touches will bloom.

Make your heart then the "rain clouds" through which Love pours into the parched world. I promise you absolutely that all that your Love touches, seen and unseen, will bloom. Conscious or unconscious. You need not name those to be blessed by your Love, though you can of course. Just know that everything in your vicinity and anyone and anything whose lives have ever touched yours will be blessed. Thus the past is healed. Old relationships are given closure. Past wrongs are righted, and all slights forgiven. Time does not exist in Love. Thus everything that touches you is touched by your Love. Past, present, future life embodied and life in spirit. In this way the world is made whole.

It is not difficult. But it takes a strength of

conviction you do not yet know you have. It is this that I call you to find, for I call your hearts back to the now – that the world of our creation be given wings and the gift of your existence be acknowledged. I promise you that there is no greater honor than that of being human. None. Not anywhere in all the heavens, in all the billions of possibilities, worlds within worlds, dimension within dimension – all the glorious and amazing life I could imagine. In all of it only you are My children. Only you have a heritage of Love that can connect the stars and embody the worlds, touch the angels and give life to a seed of creation on any level.

How can this be true, you wonder, especially as you look at the world? It is true because only you are given the choice not to love Me! Only you can turn away. For even in such turning, we are both grown. I am able to see the "depths" as well as the heights within My possibilities, and you are given the sweet, tender, exalting experience of coming back to Me, because you are able to turn away.

In this New World you will able to see. You will shed the ego, your temporary tool for individualization. Now you can choose to unfold your Love, to open your heart. You can choose at last to fulfill your destiny. And everything else, all that has made up your world will be brought back to its perfect, for everything bends to your Will. Thus all you see in this world is only that way because you chose it! As soon as you choose your true identity, everything around you resolves itself into its true identity, which is the reflection of you. As I Am the Love that enlivens all Creation, you are the Love that enlivens your world. Thus, when your Love is pure, your world is pure.

The call now goes out to your heart. Come home to the truth, home to who you are, home to the Love that is your real identity. As you respond, everything will change. Everything you thought you knew, every single definition of the world, every interaction and every form of communication will change, for the heart will then be in communion and there can be no deception there.

It will be easy. As you make your choice for Love, suddenly it will be obvious what does not fit. Words of separation and judgment will be bitter in your mouth. Separation from all you love will be agony. Any blemish to the world's beauty will be an unbearable offense. Any interruption to the sanctity of the natural world will cry out to you. Your heart will be called into action by anything unrighteous, meaning anything not based in Love. As the dialogue of Love progresses, you will be exhilarated and astounded by the intense beauty around you. Everything your awareness rests upon will naturally unfold before your gaze, revealing to you its deepest heart of hearts, its most precious truth. Understanding the honor of that revelation, you will bow down in awe at the glory of life unfolding.

Do not waste a moment! Do not waste a moment before you decide to love. Do not hesitate before saying "Yes!" to My call. For though you may not know where Love will take you, you know you will be home. You know that any reality that is not the passionate commitment to Love, that is not dedicated to honor and respect, that is not seen with the perfect vision of the heart is not a reality in which you want to dwell.

Commit yourselves! Oh, My children, you are the living proof of My trust in Love! For I believe in you enough to say, "you can choose not to love. You can choose to turn away from Me." Now you have enough information to make your choice. You now have seen both a reality of Love and a reality without Love. Without a knowledge of darkness you did not know your choice. Without your journey into separation, you could not know if you want to be joined. Without fear you have no contrast to Love. And without these lives in Time and Space, you would have no awareness of eternity.

But now – now you have separated from Me and journeyed forth. You have sharpened your ego and defined yourselves individually. You have seen the contrast of darkness and light, and in it all, because of it all, you have grown into maturity. Born of My own heart, and still beating within it like the cells of My own being, through your journey you have gained a strong enough individuality that when you return, together we will create the world. In you I know myself. In you I see all My possibilities, possibilities I had not imagined. In you I am expanded, deepened. In you I am surprised. For you, children of My being, pieces of My own heart, in your Love and imagination the world is created differently.

Only in relationship can we see ourselves, and this includes Me! Thus, in My relationship with you I come to know Myself. This then is also true for you. Both in your relationship to Me and to each other, you are granted self-awareness. This is why you must love deeply that you may see the truth of your own Love. Love with awareness that all life gains awareness through you. Look into the eyes of your beloved, into the eyes of nature, into the eyes of the angels and each time you will be revealed to yourself more deeply.

This is an expanding creation. It is not meant to stay the same. So in the joy of your creativity, the world is expanded, the universe is grown and I am enlarged. In your Love, everything is blessed and in you all things are made new.

It is time to choose. Choose to love with more passion, more dedication, more joy and more awareness. Choose this again each moment, every moment deeper than the one before. As you do, Creation blossoms around you and nourishes you so that you can again choose to love.

Love cannot enter uninvited.
Because you are living
in the world of separation,
any void will be automatically filled.
What you do not yet understand
is how actively you must make this choice
to fill your heart.
Not only when you happen to remember.
You must set up ways
to actively choose to fill your heart
until every level of your consciousness
is making this choice
continually.

Living In Abundance

I am here with you, holding you in the light, showing you the riches and the beauty of the real world — the world of Love.

Money is an illusion. It is the "coin of the realm" in the land of the ego. When you reach to Me for understanding, I want to show you something different — the new currency. It is the currency of light, which is the energy of moving Love. It is as real in the realm of the heart as money is in the realm of the ego.

Remember that in Creation it is Love directed by Will or vision that becomes form. Creation, or what you might call manifestation, always begins at the causal level, never the other way around. So form or materiality gathers around the causal energy as iron filings are drawn around a magnet.

Because money, the idea and the energy, is fraught with what you would call "baggage," it is very hard for you to see clearly. The struggle over money is created, significantly, by the belief that money is a spiritual "blockade," an impediment to getting where you want to go. All of Christiandom is tainted by an idea that is not a reflection of reality — the passage that says it is easier for a camel to get thru the eye of a needle than a rich man to get into heaven. What does this mean? Where is the sense of this? I want you to have everything. You are children of the CREATOR OF EVERYTHING! Why on Earth or in Heaven would I ever want you to live in lack?

No, dear ones, this is an insidious lie. Yes, I am contradicting the Bible and I will do this many times. As in this or any inspired message, it is only as clear as the messenger. Believe me, the Bible has been completely overhauled by those who had the ego in mind rather than the heart.

So, for those not yet able to feel the energy behind these words, I will tell you that this comes passionately. Forcefully. I want you to have abundance, and glory. I want you to reach out your hand and before it stops moving, it will be holding what you wanted. I want blessings to spring up around you, nourishment on every level to fill you — nourishment of soul and of spirit as well as of body. I want you to be surrounded by comfort, and everywhere you look you will see support, Love, and fulfillment.

In order to do this, you must believe in what I want for you. You must find your heart. You must look at your heart's deepest truth. Not your ego, but your heart. What do you see? You see a wish that everyone could be cared for perfectly, that every child be born to plenty, that poverty be a thing of the past. Now I want to tell you this. If you magnify your longing a billion times, you will touch the edge of My wishes for you. Your heart is a piece of Mine, but it is hidden from you in the fog of Time. My heart is the Love that creates you, supports you, holds your existence within it. There is nothing I would not give to you that is for your great and glorious good.

So if this is true, why is there poverty? Why are there these horrors of lack? Why are there people starving while others have money enough to feed everyone? Because you are creators, creating with your ego. This scenario is yours, dear ones, not Mine. You can rail against Me and even say you don't believe in Me because I let this happen, but the truth is that everything you see is the lie of the ego creating separation. Yes, that again.

The belief that some people have and others do not is the result of your growing up "outside of the Garden." It is the outward manifestation of this separating belief that causes this poverty. It is the belief in the existence of lack that causes the struggle over money. It was the justification of this scenario that created that supposedly divinely ordained proclamation about the needle and the camel. If this lack was meant to be holy, then why would Jesus, with a wave of his hand, provide abundance for everyone present? Because he knew he was My progeny and that all things belong to you.

With a wave of your hands, you too can create all you need. You can create loaves and fishes. You can also create money. You can manifest directly, or indirectly, as you please. I am calling you home, into the realm of your heart, and another "piece" of this awakening is the attraction of Love. When your heart is open and you are giving, that flow of energy creates a "vortex" that draws in energy from the heart level, or what you would call the spiritual plane. That energy, or light, provides you with two things — 1) energy for you to direct to form, into your manifestations, and 2) a vibrational level that, like that magnet, automatically attracts good. It will attract things into your life that vibrate at that level, the level of the heart.

If you are giving but it is from the ego, it does not set up this vortex of energy. So it is very important that the giving forth be from your heart purely. When this is the case you can know that all that is right for you on your heart level will be drawn to you.

Now, listen carefully. You must be very careful not to send it away! If you are the creative force and your good comes rushing toward you, if you believe you should not have that good for whatever reason, you actually turn it away. This happens continually. Someone will do something prompted by their true heart, an act of giving forth their spiritual energy as a blessing to another. This sets the vortex in motion. Light pours through and more light is drawn to them and — it reaches a wall of disbelief. A wall of doubt, fear, lack or belief in the "unspiritual" nature of money, and the good is turned away. Whatever trickles through the wall can only fuel the limited forms available in that person's world, where they will allow good.

"Impossible!" you say. "Everyone wants to have good and abundance." I ask you, really? What if that good tears apart your entire reality? What if that good would make everything you believe about yourself invalid? And (a big one here), what if that good challenges your entire spiritual reality? And what if it also contradicts your view of the world and your emotional experience, your "stability"?

Let me tell you the answer. You would turn it away. So this is what I must ask of you. I ask you to be willing to give up your entire knowledge of reality, how you believe the world works, who you think you are, everything, in order to accept your good.

Can you do this for Me? Can you have this much faith that you can walk through the world and not believe what it tells you? Not believe that poverty could suck you down any moment, that tragedy could be around the corner, that if you choose abundance you will lose your spiritual life? Will you give all of this up for Me?

For some this will be easy, but for others, it may be the most difficult thing you have done — because the ego's lie of separation, lack, pain, chaos and unworthiness is all you have ever known. I want you to believe in your abundance completely. Just as I ask you to choose Love, I also ask you to choose abundance. For, dear ones, it is time to come back to the Garden. The Garden of your creation, your true home, in which all that you need surrounds you, in which you reach out your hand and what you need is there. Your natural state (represented in the Bible by being naked or innocent). As I have said before, the knowledge of "good and evil" is the world of separation, dichotomy, ego.

The miracles of Jesus were glimpses of your natural state. Now because your consciousness is everything, please translate thoughts of money into thoughts of energy. Realize that every time you align yourself with your heart, when you can feel that living light within you, you are connected to that vortex which pulls into your life the energy or vibration of your greatest good.

Please begin to look at everything you do, all you give, and all you receive in this light. What are you giving forth and from what level? Is it on the level of the heart? If it is not, you must modify what you do or change what you do until it represents a true giving forth of your heart's energy. Then you can expect your good, your abundance, to come to you. Carefully observe whether you allow it in!

Now one more VERY important thing. Even those of you who believe that I provide for you usually have a very limiting belief. You believe I provide just what you need — and usually at the last minute, after I've "tested your faith" to the max, as you say. Then you squeak by and have to "have faith" again! First, it is not that I provide. It is your natural state and it is total abundance. It is being cared for as if you are the most important, most beautiful, most holy being in the universe (because you are!) How would such a being be provided for? With everything. With plenty and more than plenty. With lavish abundance! The children of God! How would such beings live? In Heaven! In the Garden of Eden. In joy and perfection.

It is only in the realm of illusion, of the separation of the ego, that lack can exist. In the real world of your heart, you only have things that vibrate at the level of Love. When you open your heart, then you must expect this good. Take a moment to allow this to penetrate. While you do, let Me tell you this: every angel, every animal, every element, every molecule that coalesces into form — all these things are here to support you in your good.

For the time being, switch to a dialogue of energy. An examination of energy. Then, when you must look at money, look through eyes that see the abundance around you. Eyes that see unlimited capacity for the manifestation of your good. As with everything you are learning, you will begin to see the ways in which you cooperate in the creation of a limited reality. You'll begin to see how you block your good. Seeing this, you will joyfully shed these old beliefs, allowing them to effortlessly fall away from you. Then you will stand, free of the illusion, ready to reclaim your heritage.

Do not accept anything less than what you know I would give to you. God to child of God. Creator to co-creator. Then you will have a way to measure your current reality against the true reality that you are meant to claim. Dear ones, I would never give you anything else! Even your individuation did not need to be like this, but you have believed the siren song, the seduction of the illusion of power instead of the truth of Love. You could have traveled easily out of the Garden and back again, but you believed an invented shadow and gave it life (being the co-creators you are.) You have been "lost in the desert" ever since.

But now the sun is so bright even the cloud cannot conceal it any longer! Let it push away the shadow. Let it warm you and bless you. Now that this light is here, please don't go chasing the shadow! The gates to the Garden are in front of you. Welcome back.

*Your mind must be directed by you
and by your Will to choose Love
in absolutely everything.
Only so are you turning
your beautiful faces homeward.*

The Question of Feeling One's Feelings

Everything is vibration. Love is the substance of creation. Everything is made from Love. Life is movement. So everything in Creation is moving Love — dancing particles of Love vibrating in joy equals life. The rate at which Love moves or vibrates is how it manifests.

Love moves so fast filled with My joy that when I created you, I could not get you to "stay away" from Me. As you know, My objective was to give life to pieces of My own heart imbued with My consciousness so you could look at Me. So I could be seen. So I could share Creation. So I would not be alone, surrounded with expressions of My Love and joy but without a consciousness that could reflect Myself back to Me and a consciousness who could expand Me.

The overwhelming joy of My thought of you would make things vibrate even more intensely. So I would will you to "be," but you would come rushing right back to Me. I realized you had to have a way to develop an individual consciousness. So I created the "pocket" of this Earth/Time/Space creation and placed you here to "gestate" and to develop as separated identities. I created a space of slower vibration so that you could maintain separation from Me.

Another way to express this is that at the high vibration of pure light that is My being, you can't resist the bliss of reunion with Me, because you remember it. You know that is who you are. And thus, you "melt" right back into Me. In order to individualize, you had to forget who you are. It was the only way it would work.

This pocket of slower vibration has indeed provided a wonderful place for you to grow. It has given you a safe arena for testing your intelligence and your co-creative abilities. As you know, this "pocket" of Time also kept the rest of Creation safe from the effects of your budding yet uncontrolled co-creative abilities.

Now I have been telling you it is the time of awakening. Time to remember who you are. Assisted by your ego you have gained individual identity. It is time to "be born," out of the womb of Time and into the realm of true reality.

The question raised is about feelings. At the lower vibrations created here to allow you to grow, things exist that do not exist in reality. In reality you are beings of great joy. There is no way I can express this to you while you are separated by the veils of Time. But as you focus in your heart, you will feel it. Exaltation. Pure joy. Excitement. Exhilaration.

Oh, beloved ones, you do have emotions, for emotions are energy in motion. They do give texture to your world. They give a depth of being. But what I have, what I Am, is an incredible and glorious depth and breadth of life. On those rare days when you feel vibrantly and perfectly alive, you have a tiny taste. It is an exhilarating anticipation of amazing goodness.

Unbelievable Love. Astounding beauty. Peaks and valleys of emotion are only different shades of exhilaration, joy and bliss. *So you do have a true emotional element. It is millions of variations of joy.*

However, as the vibrations of emotion are slowed, and slowed and slowed some more — when you are cut off from your natural joy by the terribly slow movement of things in this "womb of Time" — joy slowed down so much becomes the opposite. This is like seeing a reflection in a pond. Everything is there but it is reversed. Thus, sadness is born.

It is this sadness that is the reason your sojourn here was interpreted as "being thrown out of the Garden of Eden." Certainly it feels this way. Every other natural and real emotion, when slowed down too much becomes only a reflection of what it is meant to be. The feeling of joyous movement that is life becomes agitation and anxiety. In other words, all the things that you believe are your "natural emotions" are a reverse reflection of what you really have.

Then, to add to the challenge, the ego — your tool for individualization— manipulates this lower energy to create many variations on what is already very low energy. It creates friction by creating clashing ego energies, and anger emerges. Translated vibrationally again, when you reach the level of heartfelt feelings, you are up to the vibrational level of what is real. Expressed as chakra energy, it is heart chakra or above that is real.

So if you choose to feel grief, sadness, fear, etc.,

you may. But so choosing, it will never heal you. The idea that focusing on negativity can ever create anything positive is the most ingenious lie of the ego. Negativity will always create more negativity. Dear ones, *everything in the universe follows the law of vibrational attraction.* Whatever you have, whatever you choose, the sum of those vibrations is what will be attracted to you.

You can experience your grief, but it will not heal you. Not only that, it will keep happiness away, because what you feel, the vibration at which you choose to live is what you draw more of. We have come to a point in your evolution where you must break through the illusions of separation that has been you reality. The ego is no longer "your friend."

Only spirit can heal you. Only Love can free you. Only the choice to let go of the illusion will allow you to see the truth. This is what I give you here — glimpses of the truth so you can begin opening your heart. Dear ones, when you reach the level of the heart, reality will open before you. You will understand the truth that you are timeless beings of Love, living in a loving, alive universe, supported tenderly and joyfully by Me and by every other part of all of Creation.

You will see that you absolutely create the world you see. You will see that no one is ever lost to you. The veil of Time is an illusion. The moment you can really function in the real world you will see everyone and everything that you believed was lost to you. There will be no more grief, for there will be no loss.

So rather than spend your time playing the games of the ego, please focus on opening your heart! For truly, what you really want is Love. I promise you this. And, when you wake, you will see all of this for what it is — reflections of what you believed as you were learning who you are. You believe Love can hurt you. So it seems to. But in truth it never ever will. Love will save you. It will free you. It will bless you. It will heal you. All the rest is a lie! Oh dear ones, if you believe nothing else, believe this!

Say "yes" to love! Look fear in the face and recognize it. It is the ego's tool for keeping you from Love. Say "yes" to Love, and trust that one moment of real Love will do more to heal you than a lifetime of therapy will. Let go, dear ones. Pry your beautiful fingers away from the rocks of illusion that hold you down. Let go and let Love sweep you up in the "river of light," the movement of Love that is real life. Let joy touch you. Do not be afraid. The ego has whispered that joy will annihilate you (you see how it can "twist" the truth? How again it is a reflection, backwards, of the truth?). And, in the beginning it could. But you are beyond that now. You can hold your individuality. You can come back to Love now. Come back to Me.

Everything you believe is manifested before you. Sometimes it is subtle. Sometimes you don't see it. But what you believe is drawn to you impeccably. Personally. In form, vibrating at the rate of the sum of all your beliefs. Change your beliefs and you change your world.

Everything in this "reflected" reality was never

meant to be permanent. As you grow in your individuality, you will naturally remember who you are. You will speed up your vibration. You will open your heart. You will reclaim the real world, leaving the "womb" behind. Thus we agreed on both timing and trajectory as you moved forth from My heart.

Because everything you believe is manifested before you personally, it is in your personal relationship that you will find true Love, experience true Love, awaken into true Love. Then together you will look and see the beauty of the dance you did, the steps you took, and the story you created on the "stage of Time."

You are always with Me, and you are always with the one who is your mate. You can require them to "change before your eyes," time and time again, as you search to believe in their reality. There is no way to explain this to you at this point. All I can say is *as long as you believe you are still searching for Love, than you will continue to search. Stop and believe, and Love will manifest before you.* Love personified is your SoulMate. It is the most holy, most powerful relationship in all Creation except for your relationship with Me — and, it is your relationship with Me that it reflects.

The world is not solid, dear ones. It is only light moving so slowly that it appears to be solid. The light is speeding up. Your birth into real life is nearing. If you resist the light, it will take tremendous energy, more and more of it to hold your illusion in place. Let go, then, quickly, to everything you believe. Let your heart teach you the truth. And when it manifests Love in front of you, for heaven's sake (literally) do not turn away!

Listen with your hearts, dear ones, for your heart speaks to you in the language of reality. Love is your truth. Your heart will affirm this as soon as you are willing to accept the truth.

Dear ones,
you can't even conceive the great power
of SoulMate Love.
It can create anything you can dream of.
It can easily free you
from the confines of selfishness.
I tell you that true Love
can change everything,
and it must!

All of your life you have waited for
the touch of true and tender Love
and the ensuing ecstasy.
Now, at last,
it is beginning to happen to many of you.
This is how it is going to be
for every single human being
as each accepts the Love he or she is,
and draws the SoulMate.

True SoulMate Love Is Your Destiny

I am here, My beloved humanity. I am here,
holding you perfectly in Love. In that Love is your
perfection. In that Love is your fulfillment. In that
Love is the gift of your awakening to who and what you
are. In that Love lie the answers to every question that
has plagued humankind – every doubt, every confusion,
every pain. All the disillusionment. All of those things
that have ever made humans pause and say, "but if God
loves us, how is it possible that such negativity
would exist?"

Now it is time for you to remember Love, to
turn your precious faces back to Me. As My Love lifts
you and warms your hearts once again, dear ones, you
will know effortlessly all of the answers. The moment
you say "yes" to Love, the moment you allow the warm
sun of Love to thaw the frozen core of fear within you,
it will be obvious. It will be obvious from that moment
that you have been playing in the shadows. It will be
obvious that it could only exist – the injustice and pain
– because you were living on less than you were ever
meant to be.

Do you know how a watch begins to do crazy
things when the battery is running out? Suddenly, it
starts running minutes randomly, blinking, changing
times and making no sense. This has been the case with

humanity now for far too long. Why? Because fear and ego have had My beloved children turned away from Me. Away from Love. Away from the light that is your energy source. Away from the knowledge of your identity. With the loss of that knowledge, you were cut off from the source of your life, the energy that fuels you. You were cut off from Love.

Now, My beloved ones, I am turning your precious eyes homeward. I am calling to you and you cannot resist because Love is your nature, as it is Mine.

I want to tell you some important things. The first: I am very proud of you. I am proud that even though you were running on so little energy, even though you were facing away from the sun of My Love, even though the ego has been ruling the world, your hearts still belong to Me.

I want you to feel the blessedness of your true state, beloved ones. Quickly. I want you to realize that I have never ever doubted, even for an instant, that your hearts were Mine. I have loved. I have waited. I have watched as you grew into strong individuals, for this was always our plan. We did not expect, you and I, that so much would happen to pull you in directions away from Me. We knew it would be challenging – but because of your important free will, there were choices to be made that none could foresee.

We agreed, then, as we still agree now, that together we would be Love — Love as The All (Me), and Love as the movement into new, expanded, delightful things (you!). And when this time came as the millennium approached, all that I trusted was proven to Me, for those who could see, promised their assistance to those who could not, that all of you could turn your faces back to Me.

I say this to you to express My total Love for you. I also offer you, through the truth of your being, the doorway through which you can easily step to reclaim your full measure of Love immediately. You can reclaim the energy — the light that will fuel you and bring you back to your full capacity. I offer you the gift of transforming all that must be balanced from things you have done while facing the shadows. This doorway, this key, this answer to your questions is giving love to your SoulMate.

What a strange thing to say, you may be thinking. Of all the great possibilities for changing your life, of the thoughts mankind has entertained about repentance, karma, salvation and spirituality, how could this be the answer? Especially, you say, because very few people have their SoulMate! So does this mean that God is a tease? That I offer a grand opportunity only to reveal that it is only available to a tiny portion of humankind? These questions, I will answer.

My beloved humanity, absolutely every energy that exists in Creation is embodied at every level. Every galaxy is a grand and glorious being, within whom all that is within that system, lives and moves. That being does as I do, and lovingly guides all that is within, as all that is within grows and expands that being. Your solar system is embodied; your Earth is a living being. Even Nature is clear and loving conscious beings holding the energy for a particular plant, or species, or energy. Thus is Love also embodied at every level of every reality. Love is embodied as humanity most profoundly, because you are, literally, the cells of My heart. You are My progeny. You were made in My image and likeness. Dear ones, this is true. Thus you are the embodiment of Love.

To some of you this is a review. To others it is a first awakening. Regardless, it is very important that you keep this in front of you daily, hourly, for in so doing you will be granted your awakening. It will come in ever deeper experience of this truth. In ever wider range in your life as you expand your capacity to say "yes" to your truth.

So I say to you now that it is imperative that you open your heart, your mind, and your spirit to the proof of Love in your life. I ask you to understand that Love must be standing in front of you, as soon as you remember who you are, as you turn your beloved faces back to the light of My presence. As above, so below. As within, so without. So Love will manifest in your life, as will all good things that you embrace in your consciousness. The way to jump start this process is to understand the other fundamental of Love. *Love is always given. That is the nature of Love.*

Dear ones, it is My nature to pour forth Love — to pour Myself ever outward in an expansion of Love that has created all that exists. For Me to have held back would mean nothing would exist. It was the urge to move outward in an expansion of Love, to find more ways to Love, to create a living experience of Love being given forth, that is the essence of creation. Knowing this, dear ones, you know the truth of your own nature. My heart is the outreach of Love. It is Love giving forth. And you are My heart. Thus, dear ones, what you really are is Love seeking ways to give of itself.

I have explained to you that the embodiment of Love in your life is your SoulMate, the reflection to you of who you are, and the way by which you are meant to see yourself. Knowing now that you are made of the energy of Love being given, moving forth to bless, reaching out to shower yourself on all that is, then you can see the answer to the search. *To be true to yourself, to be what you are meant, you must be giving Love forth every moment.*

Dear ones, you will come to find that giving Love is the key to the awakening of humanity. It is as essential as the blood going forth from your heart to nourish the cells of your body. Giving Love is what will nourish your spirit. And since you are, together with your SoulMate, a cell of My heart, when Love goes forth from you, then My heart is healthy. If My heart is healthy, dear ones, it means that all Creation is healthy, for within Me is everything.

You are far bigger than you think. You have been tucked away in Time to create safely, for you and for the rest of creation, as you experimented with your power as forces of creation, your energy as the heart of All That Is. And while it may seem that you have made very large mistakes, that you have turned away *en masse* and done many horrible things, I offer you this awareness. It has only been a little while in the vast expanse of all eternity. And it has only been here, in this protected place, that you have played "cowboys and Indians" and "rich man, poor man" and "good cop, bad cop," and especially pretended you were unable to give.

And while you have heard life on Earth compared to watching a movie, you have yet to understand how easily you can now leave the theater. All you have to do is remember who I am and you will instantly know who you are. The lights will go on; the movie will be revealed, and as you leave the theater, you will do two things. You will take your trash with you and dispose of it, and, as you leave the theater, you will recognize your SoulMate. You will understand that you are one being with two parts. You will begin to give Love to your SoulMate, then and there. The moment you do, you become a healthy cell in My living heart. Then, as you continue to awaken, you will become a functioning heart yourselves, nourishing your own creation. And of course you are aware that a heart can nourish nothing unless it always and forever gives.

One of the first realizations in the awakening of humanity is the critical distinction between the ego and the heart. The moment people make this switch, they have reclaimed themselves. They have left the theater. They have begun to come alive in Reality. With every decision to choose the heart, they are reconnected with the truth of their being and with the truth of My being – who I am, who they are, and how it changes everything to realize this. It truly changes everything. The shift from getting to giving is the next big shift.

In some ways it could be said that this is the same thing – shifting from ego to heart and from getting to giving. In one sense this is true, for certainly the ego is completely focused on getting and the nature of the heart is to give. But, I must tell you now that they are not at all the same thing, because the law of giving is the law of creation. It is the absolute foundation of All That Is. It is in giving that the movement of creation is revealed, accepted, and lived. The truth of creation is Love. The movement of creation into form is giving. Thus without giving, nothing in form would have manifested.

Keep this in mind for future awakenings — that it is only in giving that you can create.

Now as Love is accepted as truth, and the heart becomes the center of your perception, your full being will be embodied. Your SoulMate will become embodied before you. *The foremost thing, even before you can actually physically see him or her, is to begin to give Love to your SoulMate.* Open your heart and pour forth Love. As you do, you establish your circulatory system in form. You begin the flow of energy from the heart that you are together. The moment you do this, and the life blood of your being (which is Love) begins flowing, your truth, the wholeness of your being begins to come alive. At this moment you know that every dream you have ever dreamed about Love, every fantasy you have ever had about your ideal relationship, is nothing compared to this reality. In this moment, as you give real Love, real Love automatically comes back to you. This, too, is a law – what you give you will receive.

I promise you, no matter how your life has been, that true SoulMate Love is your destiny. I promise you that in one moment of connection to your SoulMate, if you can be fully present, all of your doubt and all of your fear will fall away. And I also promise you this. I now bring forth the return to your wholeness, the truth of your being. It is time. So now, in this time of the turning, everything on Earth now supports the truth of Love, the reunion of SoulMates. What has taken those before you a lifetime to accomplish, you can accomplish with one call for your SoulMate, because it is time, and because those before you have cleared the path that you might walk it easily. It is time for the Golden Age, time for My beloved children to awaken from the dream, or to step out of the theater.

All that was difficult can now be easy. Yet there is a bottom line. That bottom line is your free will, for you will forever have this. It is the gift of your co-creatorship. Thus, you must ask for the truth of who you are to be embodied in your life. You must ask for your SoulMate, to experience the amazing gift of a shared heart and a reflecting consciousness.

As you give forth Love, your system of energy, or circulation, will strengthen within, or between, you. Then it will nourish absolutely everyone and everything that comes into contact with you together, and it will nourish your creations. All you have to do is join your energy systems, for light, which is the SoulMate double helix, and for Love, which is your truth as a heart of creation in your own right. Whatever "mold" you create together with your joint Will will be brought to life.

Please! Do everything you can to understand the truth of this. Please read these words. Please open your hearts. Please trust in the truth of Love. And please vow, with the great power and gifts that are yours, to serve the awakening of all of humanity. The truth of who you are means this. *It will take very few awakened SoulMates, relative to the whole of humanity, to set in motion the revolution of Love that will awaken everyone.* It will take very few SoulMate couples, who know the truth of who they are, to get the blood pumping fully, in a glory of life and awakening, through all of My heart – meaning all of humanity. The truth of Love will spread quickly. The giving of Love will nourish everything.

What had seemed missing as humanity played in the shadows, and My heart became dangerously low on energy, will quickly be reversed. But it will take commitment, especially on the part of those who are the first wave, the forerunners of the awakening. It will take turning around completely — breaking away from the mesmerizing movie, having the courage to leave the theater and to trust there is a whole new world beyond the darkened room and the movie screen. It will take strength — strength to pull away from the false reality. Strength to refuse the seduction of the ego, the senses and most of all, the habits of feeling. These are old pathways in the brain of humanity. It will be up to you to establish new pathways. It is only the repetition of truth and the request for assistance that will make this possible.

Beloved ones, you are the embodiment of Love in its perfection. The positive and the negative, the two halves that make the whole. Perfect masculine and perfect feminine energies of Christ. Christ is the name of the Love pouring forth from My joyous movement of creation, the moving forth of the Love in My heart. Thus, as SoulMates you will embody these energies that you are also able to create.

Begin giving Love to your SoulMate now. With all that you are. With every bit of your capacity, all of your will. You will feel the response. You will feel the response more and more clearly, the more you send forth. Even if your SoulMate is not in your life, he/she will respond to you. The connection will be made. Continue to do this and you will develop communion with your SoulMate. You will be able to begin your work together even if they are not embodied yet in front of you.

As you give Love to your SoulMate, you are giving forth to the world in the very most powerful way, because as soon as the two of you are fully connected, you can begin to assist with the larger awakening, together.

In Love, all that is not Love is consumed. Easily. Lovingly. There is no better way to elevate humanity, to heal or transform all that is not Love, to awaken My cherished children, than to become the heart of creation, to become My awakened children and, by the beautiful power of your Will guiding your Love, to bring all back to Me.

Your heart will testify to the truth of your SoulMate. The response to your giving Love will prove this even further. Then, as you give, you will receive and as you receive you will be wrapped in a Love so pure, so true, so familiar, so perfect, that all you can do is open your heart. When you truly open your heart, you will see your SoulMate there, right in front of you — manifesting in your life – as someone new perhaps, or being at last visible in one who is with you, who your ego probably told you could not possibly be your SoulMate. But the ego, once your ally, blocks your vision now, so that you will be amazed by what you see when you can open your heart.

Dear ones, I ask you to remember that giving Love is a law of creation. It is the truth of right relation, of energy flow, and it is the key to receiving Love. The world of illusion will insist this is backward, that you must always be looking for how to "get what you want, deserve, or need." It is a lie. It is the reverse of the truth and it closes your heart.

If you are in a relationship, if you can begin giving, even if your partner cannot, your giving will open his or her heart. It may take a little time, depending on how much your Love has to clear and transform. But it will happen. And I will guide you. I will assist you. The energy and light and all beings who embody this, will all be working to assist you. If you turn partially from illusion to truth, from shadows to the light, you will find yourself confronting the illusion held within you. So if it is being difficult, turn all the way around into the light.

It is possible to do it the other way, but it is no longer necessary. The world at large is still facing the shadow while being flooded with incoming light. Thus, all that is held in secret is being revealed and will need to be loved into freedom. But for all who can hear this, if you embrace the light fully, with passionate commitment and continual use of Will, the light will quickly become all you see. Then you are ready, with your SoulMate before you, to use your power, fueled by your Love, as the co-creators you are — to use your Love to free the rest of My beloved children, that Love will quickly become all that you see collectively.

Say "yes" to Love quickly and Love will become all that you see. Then you will be able to see all of humanity in the truth of their being and thus reinforce the truth every moment. It is a glorious time to come Home, dearest ones — a glorious time to turn fully to Me.

To The Reader

If you have resonated strongly with what you have just read, please know that there are several other books in the *Say "Yes" to Love series for you to explore. In God Unveils SoulMate Love and Sacred Sexuality,* we learn about new levels of the SoulMate relationship and its latent atomic power as a transformational force in our world. *God's Guidance to LightWorkers* expands our vision of who we are as beings of Love and directs us on the spiritual journey which continues sequentially in *God Leads Humanity Toward Christ Consciousness* and *Giving Birth to the Christ Light.*

On the pages that follow are three powerful personal communications to each of us, given through the Messages from God. If you *Make a Personal Commitment to God,* we have been assured that you will have a visible, tangible, personal experience of God. *Dissolving Impediments to Opening the Heart* came as a meditation. It is given to assist us in releasing any blocks to an open heart and to accelerate reunion with our SoulMate. In response to God's request for the widest possible distribution of *A Letter from God to Humanity on Creating a World of Love,* we include it here.

We also invite you to visit our active, ever-changing Circle of Light website, www.circleoflight.net where excerpts and complete Messages from God are posted on many subjects. There is also a page of readers' questions with answers that elaborate upon the content of the Messages. You may also join our email list for a monthly Message from God.

May you live with an open heart in a world of Love every moment!

The Team at Circle of Light

You Can Have a Personal Relationship With God

Make A Commitment To God Now.

God is preparing a Net of Living Love with which to lift the world, and is asking you to be a part. In recent Messages, God said "My Love is pursuing you. My grace now comes to stand before you, harder and harder to ignore–until beloveds, it will take more strength than all the legions of the lie to keep My grace from touching you and awakening you, My heart, into the Love you are."

God asks that you **make a written Commitment to open to God** (by whatever name is comfortable for you) **and begin a daily communion with God for yourself.** We have found that a wonderful time to do this is in the morning before getting out of bed, but it may be done at any time that fits your personal life schedule. The important thing is that it is done at least once daily and with consistency.

God has promised that each person who does this will have direct experience of a personal communion with God, "as long as they keep hope alive and the living spirit connection in their life." It is each person's responsibility to keep the connection open. **"You will have all the light of Heaven coming to you."**

God has also asked that we at Circle of Light Spiritual Center act as a bridge, and each day bless and amplify every Commitment we receive, thus raising its vibration and magnifying the effect of its words. "...there will be those who begin to fly – whose hearts have wings – and they open to Me with great hunger and great joy. These we shall quickly add to the team of those who are part of the LightHouse."

God also has asked that each person make a list of the things for which they are grateful—"to include the success of their connection to Me, and a list of people to whom they wish to send My Love."

In Love, we deliver these instructions from the Messages from God as to how to proceed.

MY COMMITMENT TO GOD
How To Proceed

Please fill out both Parts I and II below, and your name, address and email address. Keep a copy of what you have written for yourself to review several times daily. Mail or email a copy of your Commitment to us so that we may amplify it at Circle of Light Spiritual Center. If you wish, you may go to our website, www. circleoflight.net to post your Commitment.

Part I
Please do use your own words but we give sample wording to assist you. You are of course not limited to what we suggest below. Be passionate; be real; speak your heart. Write in the present tense, as though what you are doing has been already accomplished. Please KNOW that as you make this Commitment, you WILL begin to have direct experiences of God.

Sample wording: "I am making a deep commitment to open my heart and call God personally into my life each day. I am taking responsibility to maintain this connection, and I ask Circle of Light to amplify it for me in every way possible."

Part II
(a) Please write a list of things for which you are grateful, including the success of the above connection you are making with God. Again use the present tense. (b) Please also list people to whom you wish God to send Love.

MAIL OR EMAIL a copy of your Commitment to:

Circle of Light Spiritual Center
3969 Mundell Road
Eureka Springs, AR 72631
connect@circleoflight.net
www.circleoflight.net

DISSOLVING IMPEDIMENTS TO OPENING THE HEART

The following Meditation on *Dissolving Impediments to Opening the Heart* was given through Yaël Powell at Circle of Light on Tuesday November 19, 2002, during a group meeting. Once you have done this Meditation and established this connection with God, there is no need to repeat it. Any and all impediments to having a clear and open heart through which God can pour Love will continue to arise, and God will continue to remove them.

You may re-experience briefly in your mind and emotions the situations that created these impediments, even with some discomfort. This is the "replay" as the removal is occurring. If this occurs, know that it is of the past, and do not be concerned. Simply pray gratitude, giving thanks for the fact that all blockages to your completely open heart are now being removed. Reading the excerpt from the Messages from God at the end of the Meditation will clarify this.

As you do the Meditation, read a paragraph, and then close your eyes and allow time to completely absorb the experience. You may want to record it on a tape and play it back to yourself.

Meditation On
Dissolving Impediments
To Open The Heart

Begin by taking deep breaths, sinking into your heart with all of your consciousness. With every breath in, open your heart, larger and larger and larger. As you breathe in and your heart opens, feel yourself connecting to the All of God, the great ocean of Love, vibrant and alive, vast, yet tender.

So now you have a gloriously open heart connected to the All of Love. The vast, the un-manifest. And now you feel that ocean of God's Love permeating your being and funneling through your heart. Not just your physical heart, of course, but the heart of Love that you are. With every out-breath, God pours through you to touch and love manifested life.

We are aware of ourselves now as that point where God loves through us. Be conscious of how it feels as Love pours through you. Feel how it blesses, how it kisses every cell of your body, how it illuminates every particle of Love that you are, how it resonates with the light that is in every atom, with the life that you are. How does it feel to be the very heart of God?

Breathe in, becoming the open heart, communing with the All of Love. Breathe out as Love pours through the opening that is you and God's Love comes into the world. Notice how it feels to be touched by this Love, to be its vehicle, its vessel. Allow the Love to pour through you and then, allow your mind to notice, AFTER the fact. Notice, if you can, how this Love honors the truth of who you are, your existence.

As you feel this Love pouring through you, keep expanding in your awareness of the heart that you are. Keep expanding until there is nothing else. No personality, no body, only the glorious opening for Love. Feel the celebration of life, exaltation, joy as that Love pours through you. Notice that there is only Love, washing through you, pouring through you, rushing through you, without discrimination. It doesn't go some places and not to others. It doesn't find some lives worthy and others not. It just pours through you. All of life manifest is being loved through us. The rushing, dancing river of living Love, pouring through the heart of God we are.

Now placing our consciousness right at that point that is the opening of our heart, the place where God's Love pours through, the window pane of our spirit – the heart – allow to rise up before this opening something that restricts the passage of this Love — something that is a belief or a part of who you think you are, something that needs the forgiveness of letting go. Allow it to rise up from within from the wisdom that God is with you. Hold it there in front of the opening that is your heart.

Now, breathing in – connect to the glorious All of the Love of God and allow that Love pouring through your heart to love that flaw, that part that needs releasing. To love it, to love it, to pour that Love upon it with passion and with tenderness, all the urgency of the river of life, reaching through to lift it up, to dissolve its hold on your heart. Love washes it tenderly until you see it dissolving, until where there was a blockage, there is only living Love. Know that anything exposed to this Love can only dissolve, its energy freed at last.

And now, breathing in, you are held within the All of God. You are held in Love so magnificent that you are filled with joy and love so tender that you are sure in every fiber of your being of God's personal support of you. You are suspended in abundance and perfection – the perfection of God's Love for you. You are resting in the ocean of God and you are filled with a clarity you have never known – the experience of how precisely God shows you your unique beauty, the truth of your creation. This glorious all encompassing, personal yet limitless Love of God reveals to you the full capacity of your heart, so that now…

Breathing out, God's Love now flows through you completely unimpeded. The opening that is the center of your being, the great heart that you are is filled with ecstasy because now you are aware that this very same tender uplifting, deeply personal Love of God you have experienced, can pour through your heart. In this way God may reach others through the sacred opening for Love that you are. The "window-pane" of your spirit, the center of your being, your heart, is crystal clear.

Breathing in, you feel the sweet support of the All of God, reflecting to you your truest self. Breathing out, you know yourself as the clear unimpeded heart through which God now perfectly loves the world. Every person, every plant, every particle of energy – God will love them through you. And as divine Love is ever moving through you, you will be giving beyond any thought or desire to receive. Just so will you truly receive all that you give, which is now all that God gives through you, multiplied and delivered to your open and accepting heart.

Now you have the assurance that all impediments will be removed from your heart by God. So you can simply rest in this assurance – that God will do the work of Love in and through you now in each and every moment.

Commentary on
Dissolving Impediments To Opening
The Heart

Excerpt from *The Messages from God*
Through Yaël Powell, Circle of Light
November 24, 2002

"The impediments before your heart, any one of you, unravel like a skein of wool when the Love hits it, and unraveling, they do 'replay' themselves. They engage the projector, pull down the screen and play a movie in your mind. For, of course, this is what life in the ego really is – billions of unraveling 'movies' playing out the mind's beliefs, over and over, as the light of My Love seeks entry.

"Yet you can know, you who now begin to come to the central point consciously, that the more you stay 'out of your mind,' the fewer 'new movies' you create, and soon (sooner than you think), there won't be any 'movie reels' left to play.

"When you say, 'Yes,' to Love, you are saying that you are willing to dissolve those impediments. To let the light of My Love into the movie theatre. Thus, for you who see your lives becoming beauty, the reflection of your heart — you can know that if suddenly you are 'in the play' again, it IS the clearing out of those things cluttering up the heart space, those things that 'push the pendulum' so that it swings away from the center point. Especially if you are choosing to accept the tools given [the above Meditation], then you can positively know this is the case, and that it won't take long and you will be able to remain in the stillness of My Love, allowing Me to live every moment through you."

A Letter From God to Humanity
On Creating A World Of Love

Through Yaël and Doug Powell
February 25, 2003

My beloved ones, humanity, I pour this to you with My tender Love, upon streams of light, to touch your waiting hearts. With it come the keys to your remembrance. The remembrance of your beauty and of all the ways I made you in My image. And remembrance of the truth of Love, how every human heart was born in Love and every human being is a child of God. And the remembrance that your heart is our connection and that through it lives your co-creative power. Through it comes your treasure; all the gifts I give to you forever. Through it you will now remember and find yourselves awaking to the truth of Love you are.

How I love you! You are truly the greatest of all miracles. You are My own heart, alive and in embodiment, ready to expand, to ever go forth to give the Love you are. You make Love vibrant, surprising, new. Only you, beloved ones, My precious glorious children, only you can go forth in breathless anticipation and see the Love I Am with a new perspective. Have you not marveled at your wonderful curiosity? At how insatiably you go forward to meet and greet the world? And how deeply you are moved by every expansion of beauty? This is the miracle of your co-creative heart.

My Will for you, all of you, every sweet magnificent golden child of God, is a world of peace and a life of plenty. By looking at Me, you can have these things.

Your heart is the source of your power, your treasure, your identity, your life. Your heart is connected to Me forever. And through your heart you will receive your blessings, the treasures of joy and Love and ever greater abundance that I have waiting for you. Oh! It is My heart's true desire to deliver to you the very keys to heaven that you may live heaven here on Earth, yes, and everywhere you are for all eternity. All that is necessary is for you to return to your heart to find the joy in life that contains the heart's true resonance and the cornucopia of every good, which shall pour forth before you as your life and your world.

I Am a God of Love, dear ones. Forever and forever. There is nothing but Love in Me. Let your heart stir in its remembrance of the great truth, for on it rests the salvation of this precious world and your thousand years of peace that, truly, goes on forever. You have known this, somewhere deep inside. You have known that I Am Love and that all of this before you did not make sense. All the wars and illnesses, the brothers turning upon their brothers, the poverty, the pain, even ageing and death. Oh, dear ones, I have heard you as you cried out in the dark night of your soul for answers. How every single one of you has asked the question, "If God loves us, why would God create children who have cancer and whole peoples who are starving; so emaciated they already look like skeletons?" It did not seem right to you. This, dear ones, was the message of your heart seeking to show you the truth. And when you have asked, "God, what is my purpose, the meaning of my life?" you have been responding to the nudging of your heart. But some, not hearing their hearts, have turned away, believing I could not be a loving parent to My children if I created such a world of horrors.

Now it is time for the truth. You are ready. And for those of you who read this and already know this, I ask you to deepen your commitment to the living of it, and to pass this on to My other precious children. For those of you who read this and find it inconceivable, I ask you to drop into a focus on your heart for a moment and just allow this to be a possibility. Then pass it on to others – that each hand, each set of eyes, each heart that comes in contact with this letter written in light may also take a moment to allow this possibility to be planted in their life.

Beloved ones, I love you. I love you with a Love as great as the very cosmos. I love you with a joy in your existence that pours forth greater in every moment. I love you as the very heart within Me. I love you, and My Love never wavers, never changes, never ever stops. I long for you to know this, to feel our sweet communion. I long to lay before you all the treasures of creation. You are Mine. Now. And Now. Forever. And nothing can ever change this. It is a fact of your existence.

I did not create this world of pain. You did. You did this when you chose to believe in good, in Love, **and** in something else, which you named the opposite of Love. Call it the moment in the Garden when you ate the fruit of good and evil. Call it the first judgment. Whatever you call it, beloved ones, it is your own creation. And you set yourselves up as being able to decide which was which and thus began this world of duality, of light *and* dark, of Love and anti-Love. But, precious humanity, I Am only Love. And living in Me, you, too, are only Love. So you had to create a false world, a pretend place where darkness could exist, because it cannot exist in that which is ever and only light, which I Am.

You have wandered in the desert of your co-creative minds ever since. For if your heart, connected to Me, knows the truth of only Love, then you had to find another way to view a dual scenario – and thus evolved the tool of your minds.

Oh, dear ones, I do not intend to go into lengthy explanations. All I come to say to you is that you are only Love. And that the more you choose to live through your heart, the more and more clearly you'll see the world as it really is. The more you will experience that true Love of God, the Love that I hold you in each and every moment.

Today you live in a world on the brink of war, a world filled with negativity and so much pain that you have to numb yourselves to survive. So you have nothing to lose by putting to the test what I now show you.

If you know that I Am only Love, then you must know that I Am ever holding for you the world of your inheritance, the world of joyous ecstasy and glorious abundance. You know that I Am not a power you can call on for overcoming darkness, for darkness is not in Me.

You know that any moment you connect with Me you connect with the Love and perfection I have always held for you and always will. I Am unchanging Love. In the truth of this Love there is no negativity.

Then what about this world of pain before you? What of the wars and rumors of wars? What of the fear and all the experiences that keep happening in your life? They are you, dreaming, beloved one. They are you lost within the million threads of possibility streaming from your decision to believe in good *and* evil. And just as you dream in the night and your dreams feel real, so it is with this world. So very real and filled with pain, it feels.

There is another way to live. It is to stand before this world of lies each morning and to choose to live in only Love. To consciously reject the illusion of the judgment that there is good and evil. To place your Will in Mine and ask that I lift you up enough that you can see the difference. The difference between the truth of Love that lives within your heart and this world of swirling negativity that is alive within your mind

And once you know that I Am Love and you are ever alive in Me, then you shall truly walk through this world in peace. When you know your home is Me and you affirm the heart, you could walk through a war-torn countryside with bombs falling all around you and know that none could touch you, and none would touch our home.

I will answer your questions. "What about the others?" your heart cries out. "What good is it if I am safe

in you, God, if all around me people are in misery?"
Beloved ones, the answer is this. As you clear the dream,
as you return your Will to Me, as you walk within the
truth of the Love we are together, then around you there
becomes an aura of peace; a great ball of light comes forth
as the living truth of Love you are becoming. At first it
may only clear *your* life of the illusion, as your faith in
Love restores you to the heaven you belong in, and as,
choice-by-choice and day-by-day, you turn to Me for your
identity and not to the world you have believed is outside
of you. But every day that light grows – exactly as would
happen if you turn on a physical light in a dark closet full
of scary shapes. The light fills every space – there is no
darkness left – and everything that seemed to be so
menacing becomes something neutral. Something you
can change by moving out the old furniture, or something
that you at least know is harmless.

Thus, as you grow in your ability to stay attuned
to Me, to choose the world that is your birthright as a
child of God, the greater the circumference of the light
that surrounds you. First it begins to light up your
neighbors. Suddenly they can see that there are no
terrifying things lurking in their lives; that they are free to
choose to be happy, to have joy. And with every moment
that you spend in communion with the truth of your
heart, the greater is that light of truth around you…until
you affect the neighborhood and then the town you live
in, and the county, then the state in which you live. Until
ultimately you will do as Jesus did: everywhere you are,
people will see their truth as Love, and knowing this with
all their heart they will leave their illnesses, their problems
and their strife behind – simply from experiencing the

power of your light as you live your life as only Love.

Then as others do the same, soon you'll walk into the world and the illusion of negativity will have to fall away. You will have "turned on the light in the theater," that which you call the world, and all who had believed life was a battle will suddenly be freed.

In your Western world, there is a passage in the Bible from he who came to show you the way to the heart's truth: "You cannot serve both God and mammon." This is exactly what it means. You cannot believe in a world of good and evil and also seek to create a life of Love. For from within the dream of duality every choice for Love contains its opposite.

Beloved ones, if this speaks to you, if something stirs within your heart (or, of course, if you cry out, "Oh, I know this!"), then you are here to show the way. Here to see My face, My Love, in every human being, no matter the part they now play within the dream of good and evil, of Love and anti-Love. You are here to build the New, to bring forth the heaven of living Love in which you are ever meant to live. Turn to Me and daily, moment by precious moment, I will show you who you are: a child of Love so beautiful that your cloak is made of stars, your heart is a living sun lighting up the darkness and revealing only light.

Give Me your Will, let Me lift you so you can see each moment the unity of Love. How all creation is My being and every part, magnificent and joyous, dances in a swirl of sweet exploding life. I will help you see beyond duality, beyond the veil within which lives the dream of separation being dreamed by My children. I Am only Love. And your heart is the key to the treasures held for you beyond time. Time – the illusory creation coming forth from "fitting into experience" a pendulum of good and bad experience.

Beloved ones, I speak to you whose hearts have known, have known deep inside that I would not create such a world as this you see before you. It can be easy to disengage, but you've lived the illusion for a long time. Thus can you assist each other in this. Assist each other in placing your attention on your hearts and using the power of Love you find there to infuse the world you want, not the world that's passing, the world of so much pain. You are co-creators. Made in My image, remember? It is true. You are made in My image and thus do you manifest the beliefs of your heart. Remember, the heart is where we are connected, so all the power, all the light, all the Love I pour to you comes directly and unfailingly to and through your heart. I Am Creator; I Am Love expanding through you.

And My covenant with you, My children, is that I shall always and forever grant your heart's desires. This is the promise given to each of you at the moment of your creation as children of the Love I Am. So if deep in your heart you are afraid, if you believe your heart is broken (pay attention to these words), if you are afraid that Love will hurt you, if you keep yourself protected, if you are waiting every moment for "the other shoe to drop," if you feel the world is hopeless, if you feel that life's not worth it, if you feel the world's about to end, be it from polluting it to death or from chaos and war, these deep "ways you feel" about your life – these are your heart's beliefs. And thus, beloved ones, **by our covenant** they shall manifest before you. For as the Love I Am comes pouring to you, whatever is held before the opening of your heart is what Love shall bring to life, shall help you co-create.

Thus you see that, if you stand before the White House with anger in your heart, with belief that nothing changes, that government is corrupt, and, worst of all, if you hold hatred there, within the temple of God that you are, then that, dear ones, is what you shall have more of.

You are the prize of the universe – the heart of God gone forth to create. There is really only Love to create with. But if you choose Love and anti-Love, you turn your face away from Love and, peering into the world you've made, you look for your identity. Oh, precious ones, don't find it there! Please wake into the truth of Love. Place your every resource with your true and glorious heart. I promise you that Love is the only power. And that, truly, it is the heart with which you shall always create what you experience, be it now, on Earth, or later, "after death." There is no progression, no good and bad, no better and best. There is only the truth of Love or the dream of separation.

If you can make this leap, you are those who bridge heaven and Earth, who begin to reclaim the paradise you never really left. But if you cannot, then please do continue on growing in your faith in Love. It is good to pray for peace, for even though it contains the belief in its opposite, for the moments you are focusing on Love you are using your co-creative consciousness to lift you ever closer to the unity of Love. It is best, however (and I use these terms because they are relevant here), it is the true way, the way that Jesus came to show you, to see only Love. To place every bit of the power of your heart upon the paradise of Love that this Earth is in truth, giving none of your energy to the illusion that I can ever create anything but Love.

Do you see? Do you see how this must be a fantasy if in Me darkness does not exist? If I Am All That Is, which I Am, then nowhere in Creation is there anything but Love. Oh, dear ones, this I promise you. You were created in Love; made as a glorious reproduction of what I Am as Creator. You thus came forth, truly, as Twin Flames, the forces of the Divine. Ocean of Love, Divine Feminine, and the great movement of My Will upon it, Divine Masculine. Born as one with two points of conscious Love, you forever exist in a grand unity of Love, sparking together to co-create more Love.

I call you home. Home to the unity of Love I Am and that you are in Me. Every thought for peace, every prayer has value, and every act of service in Love's name to another is a star in the night of this "pocket of duality." But the real service for which many of you have come is to join together, heart after heart, in the conviction of the truth of only Love and, forming a net of your great auras of light, to lift the world free of the reversal caused by humanity's belief in good and evil.

Thank you, beloved one, for reading this. Do you feel My living presence in your heart? Do you see the light behind these words, the packages of Love I now deliver? Then you are called, beloved one. Called to remember a world of only Love. Called to place this vision before you until it sinks into your heart and becomes your one desire: to return to My children their birthright. You have angels all around you. Your hands are being held, finger of light to finger of light, by the masters who go before you to pave the way. Your every affirmation of the world of Love you choose is heralded by archangels as they trumpet across the heavens, "A child of God awakes! A child of God awakes!" And choruses of beings, living stars greater than your sun, carry forth the message that the whole of Love I Am is filled with rejoicing. For every child of God who returns heals those many lives of the dreams of anti-Love that sprang forth from their creative heart. And the whole of the cosmos is glad, because a hole in My heart, caused by your facing away into "darkness," is healed. The heart of God is mended, ah, but more than this: the Love I Am goes forth again as you to create new things for us to love together.

I Am calling. You can hear Me. It won't be long now, beloved ones.

ABOUT THE AUTHORS

Yaël and Doug Powell live at Circle of Light, a spiritual center in Eureka Springs, Arkansas, that looks out over Beaver Lake and the Ozark Mountains. Both Yaël and Doug are ordained ministers, and the lovely Chapel at Circle of Light is the frequent scene of beautiful sacred weddings.

Yaël spends a good deal of her time in bed as a result of pain from a severe physical disability. Her "up-time" is spent officiating at weddings or receiving the Messages from God in meditation. Doug is an artist and skilled craftsman at pottery and woodworking. If it is windy, you'll definitely find him at his lifelong passion – sailing! Shanna Mac Lean, compiler and editor of the Messages, also lives at Circle of Light. If not at the computer, she can be found in the organic vegetable garden.

Completing the Circle of Light family are their wonderful animal companions. Christos (boy) and Angel (girl) are their two beloved Pomeranians. Ariel (Duff Duff) is a pure white cat who mostly frequents the garden. Then there is Magic Cat, who has been with Yaël for 15 years. They have a deep and very special communion. Magic Cat has been communicating messages through Yaël to assist humans to understand the Web of Life. In the future, he will have his own book, "Magic Cat Explains God!"

CIRCLE OF LIGHT ORDER FORM
SAY 'YES' TO LOVE SERIES

Please send the following:

___Copies of God Explains Soulmates @ $11 _____($3 S&H)
___Copies of God Unveils SoulMate Love & Sacred Sexuality
@ $19.95 _____($3.50 S&H)
___Copies of God's Guidance to LightWorkers @ $14 _____
($3 S&H)

Prices are for the USA. For more than one book, reduce each
S&H by $1. For postage to other countries, please email us first
and we will find the best shipping cost.

Name:_____

Address:_____

City, State:_____ Zip Code:_____

To use credit cards, please go to our web site www.circleoflight.net
OR you may fax your order with credit card to (479) 253-2880.
If it is busy, call 877-825-4448 and we will activate the fax.

Name on Card:_____

CC#:_____

Exp. Date:_____

If you would like to be on our email list and receive monthly
Messages from God, please fill out the following:

Email address:_____

Circle of Light
3969 Mundell Road, Eureka Springs, Arkansas 72631
www.circleoflight.net
Sayyes@circleoflight.net
1-866-629-9894 Toll Free or 479-253-6832, 8132